CW00631732

WORD 2003

SCOTT BASHAM

In easy steps is an imprint of Computer Step
Southfield Road . Southam
Warwickshire CV47 0FB . United Kingdom
www.ineasysteps.com

Copyright © 2004 by Computer Step. All rights reserved. No part of this book may be reproduced or transmitted in any form or by any means, electronic or mechanical, including photocopying, recording, or by any information storage or retrieval system, without prior written permission from the publisher.

Notice of Liability

Every effort has been made to ensure that this book contains accurate and current information. However, Computer Step and the author shall not be liable for any loss or damage suffered by readers as a result of any information contained herein.

Trademarks

Microsoft® and Windows® are registered trademarks of Microsoft Corporation. All other trademarks are acknowledged as belonging to their respective companies.

Printed and bound in the United Kingdom

ISBN 1-84078-263-3

Contents

1   Getting to know Word   7

Introduction   8
The Word 2003 screen   9
Page views   10
Toolbars   13
Adjusting the page setup   14
Automatic customization   15
Help   16
Using Smart Tags   18

2   Basic text manipulation   19

The Document window   20
Click and Type   24
Multiple text selection   25
Auto Recover   25
Handwriting text   26
The Task Pane   27
Saving a document   28
Opening a document   28
Print Preview   29
Printing a document   30

3   Formatting text   31

Character-level formatting   32
The Font dialog box   34
Paragraph-level formatting   36
Forms of alignment   36
Bulleted paragraphs   37
Advanced bulleting   38
Numbered paragraphs   40
Advanced numbering   41
Outline numbered lists   42
Formatting with the Task pane   43
The Paragraph dialog box   44

4 Working with a document 47

Scrolling 48
Zooming 49
The Ruler 50
Cut and Paste 50
Copy and Paste 52
The Task Pane Clipboard 53
Undo and Redo 54
Page breaks 55
Defining sections 55
Using columns with sections 56
Headers and footers 58
The Format Painter 60
Document properties 61
The Document Map 62

5 Styles and Themes 63

Using the default Styles 64
Editing an existing Style 65
Creating a new Style 66
The Style dialog box 67
Character-level Styles 69
AutoFormat 70
Themes 71
The Style Gallery 72
Displaying Style names 74

6 Using Speech Recognition 75

Preparing to use Speech Recognition 76
Dictating text 77
Entering Voice Commands 78
Correcting errors 78

7 Tabulation 79

Default Tabulation 80
Creating your own Tabulation 80
The Tabs dialog box 83
Using Tabs to create Tables 84

Automatic features   85

8

Find and Replace	86
Special characters	91
Spelling and Grammar checking	92
AutoCorrect	94
AutoText	95
The Spike	96
AutoComplete	97
Hyphenation	98

Templates and Wizards   99

9

Using templates	100
Template defaults	101
Form templates	102
Setting up a new template	105
Changing Styles in a template	106
The Templates and Add-ins dialog	106
Wizards	107

Graphical features   109

10

Inserting pictures from disk	110
Inserting Clip Art	111
Manipulating graphics	112
The Picture toolbar	113
Cropping a picture	113
Editing an imported picture	114
Wrapping text around graphics	115
The Format Picture dialog	116
The Drawing toolbar	116
Creating shapes	117
Lines and fills	117
AutoShapes	118
Changing object order	119
Grouping and ungrouping	120
WordArt	121

Tables and charts — 123

11	Inserting/Drawing a table	124
	Formatting	128
	Nested tables	130
	Formulae	131
	Borders and shading	132
	Table AutoFormat	134
	Graphics within tables	136
	Formatting a chart	138

Web-based documents — 141

12	Creating a Web document	143
	Frames	145
	The Web Tools palette	148
	Adding video clips	149
	Hyperlinks	151
	Editing existing HTML files	153

Working with others — 155

13	The Reviewing toolbar	156
	Inserting Comments	157
	Collaborating on documents	158
	Versioning	159
	Tracking changes	160
	Protecting a document	162
	Shared Workspaces	163
	Using XML	164

Advanced topics — 167

14	Text boxes	168
	Macros	169
	Footnotes and Endnotes	171
	Tables of Contents	172
	Indexing	178
	Adding sound	181
	The Research Pane	183
	Compatibility options/Installing features	186

Index — 187

Getting to know Word

This chapter quickly gets you started with Word 2003. It explains the screen layout, and introduces the various viewing modes that you can use to display your documents. It looks at new Word 2003 features such as the Reading Layout view and the enhanced Task Pane.

Covers

Introduction | 8

The Word 2003 screen | 9

Page views | 10

Toolbars | 13

Adjusting the page setup | 14

Automatic customization | 15

Help | 16

Using Smart Tags | 18

Chapter One

Introduction

Word processing was one of the first popular applications for the modern personal computer. In the early days it provided little more than the ability to enter and change text on a computer monitor. As time went on, software and hardware improved, and features such as spell-checking and visual type effects were added. The number of users increased.

Microsoft Word 2003 for Windows is widely acknowledged as a leader in its field, and is one of the best selling packages in any software category.

Let's face it, with Word 2003, we're talking about a big package. It has retained its position as market leader by stuffing itself full of useful features, taking it from word processing into the realms of graphical and data-oriented documents, and adding the capacity for easy-to-use Web publishing. At first it may seem to contain a bewildering array of options and controls, but many are there to make life easier – providing quick access to the most commonly used features.

A big package inevitably comes with a depressingly large amount of reference material, which will describe each and every function in minute detail. This book is not intended to replace Microsoft's documentation; instead you should view it as a more graphical teaching guide. Wherever possible, pictures and examples are used rather than pages of text, to explain and demonstrate the concepts covered.

To gain maximum benefit from this book:

- Make sure that you are first familiar with the Windows operating environment (using the mouse, icons, menus, dialog boxes and so on). Please refer to "Windows XP in easy steps" in the same series if necessary.

- It is important to experiment using your own examples – as with many things, you will find that practice is the key to competence.

The Word 2003 screen

Start Word by selecting Programs > Microsoft Office > Microsoft Office Word 2003 from the Start menu. You should see the following screen.

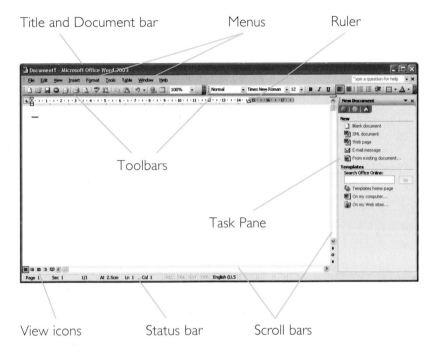

Title and Document bar — Menus — Ruler

Toolbars

Task Pane

View icons — Status bar — Scroll bars

To quickly activate a toolbar, right-click on any visible toolbar to display a shortcut menu. Check the toolbar of your choice. To deactivate a toolbar follow the same procedure, but instead uncheck the toolbar in the menu.

Don't worry if the screen you see has extra items or things missing; you'll see in a moment that it's possible to configure the Word screen in different ways.

Toolbars

Toolbars can appear at the top of the screen, at the bottom, or as floating palettes. They give you instant access to features without the need to search through menus and dialog boxes. There are twenty-one toolbars in total, but we usually only require some of them at any one time. For more on toolbars see Pages 13 and 15.

Task Pane

The Task Pane (often classed as a toolbar) is a handy pane from which you can undertake a wide variety of jobs. Its advantage is that, unlike a dialog box, it stays on-screen as long as you want – you don't have to interrupt your work to launch it.

Page views

You can select five ways of viewing a page from the View menu: Normal, Web Layout, Print Layout, Outline and Reading Layout.

Normal view

This view is effective for fast editing of text, but depicts a simplified layout – not always displaying objects such as images.

 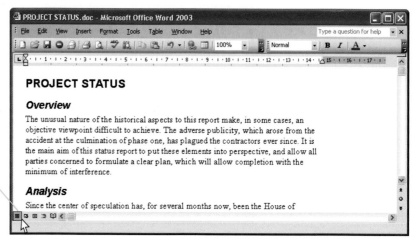

The quickest way to switch between views is to use these icons in the bottom left corner of the screen.

Web Layout view

This view shows you how your document would appear in a Web browser. Text and tables wrap to fit the window. Background images and effects are also visible.

 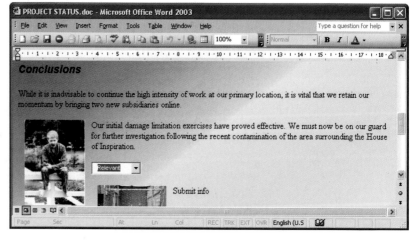

In any of these views, paragraph symbols (markers denoting carriage returns, spaces, etc.) are by default not visible. To display them, click on the Paragraph Symbols icon normally displayed in the Standard toolbar.

Print Layout view

This view displays your document as actual pages, previewing text and graphic effects.

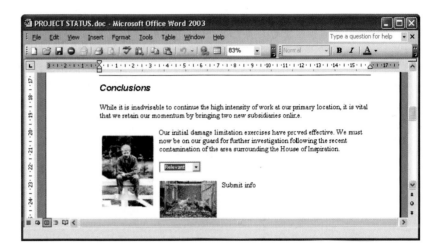

Outline view

HOT TIP

The structure of a document can be rearranged from Outline view by dragging the plus and minus signs to another position.

This allows you to view your text as a structured outline. Each major heading is marked with a plus sign; subordinate headings are marked with a minus sign. To collapse a heading so that subordinate headings are not displayed, double-click on the plus sign.

HOT TIP

To learn more about using a consistent set of headings and subheadings see Chapter 5 "Styles and Themes".

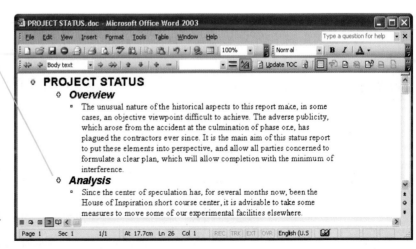

Reading Layout view

This view, new to Word 2003, provides you with the best way to read documents directly on the computer screen. Unnecessary toolbars are hidden, and Word sizes the document for maximum readability based on the screen resolution.

There are two easy ways to navigate through a document. The Document Map appears as a pane on the left of the window. You click on a heading to move straight to that part of the document.

Bear in mind that Reading Layout view could display your document very differently from the way in which it will print. In particular, text size and page breaks will tend to be different to the printed result. To see an accurate representation of your document on paper use Print Layout view.

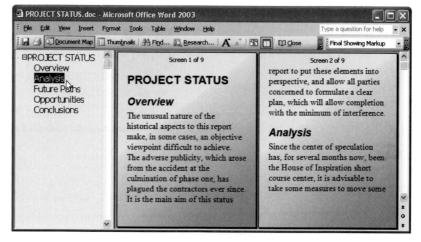

Document Map

Click the Thumbnails icon to navigate using small page images.

You can also activate the Document Map and Thumbnails in the other views.

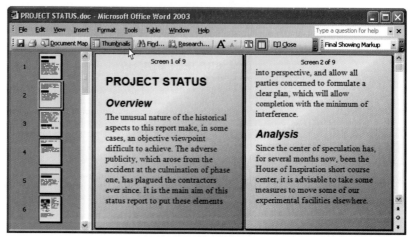

Thumbnails

Toolbars

To add a new button to a toolbar, right-click over the toolbar. Click Customize. In the dialog which appears, click the Commands tab. In the Categories field, click a category (a group of associated icons). In the Commands box, drag a button onto the toolbar in the open document, then click Close.

Toolbars are important components in Word. A toolbar is an on-screen bar which contains shortcut buttons. These symbolize and allow easy access to often-used commands which would normally have to be invoked via one or more menus.

For example, the Word Standard toolbar lets you:

- create, open, save and print documents

- perform Copy & Paste and Cut & Paste operations

- undo editing actions

- insert a hyperlink

by simply clicking on the relevant button.

Specifying which toolbars are displayed

Pull down the View menu and click Toolbars. Now do the following:

To move a toolbar, click the left edge and drag to another location. (Dragging to the main page area makes the toolbar freestanding.)

1 Click the toolbar you want to be visible – a checkmark appears against it.

2 Repeat this process to hide the toolbar – the checkmark disappears.

To resize a toolbar, drag on its right edge.

Remember that the Task Pane is a toolbar. To hide or show it, uncheck or check the Task Pane entry in the Toolbars submenu.

Adjusting the page setup

Go to the File menu and choose Page Setup. The Page Setup dialog box appears. Like many of Word's dialog boxes it is tabbed, (subdivided into sections). You can select your required section by clicking on the appropriate tab at the top of the box.

As an alternative to using the mouse, pressing Control together with the Tab key will cycle through each dialog box tab in turn.

Pressing the Alt key together with any underlined letter in the dialog box will simulate a mouse click on that particular control. For example, in the Page Setup dialog, Alt+S selects Landscape page orientation.

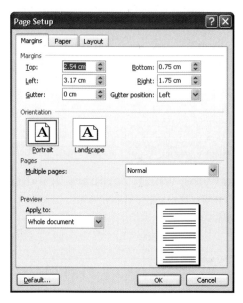

1 Make sure the Margins tab is selected.

2 Type in any required changes to the margin or header/footer dimensions.

3 Click on the Paper tab.

4 Select a paper size from the drop-down list, or enter custom values in the Width and Height boxes.

5 Make any necessary changes in the Layout tab.

6 Click OK to apply your changes.

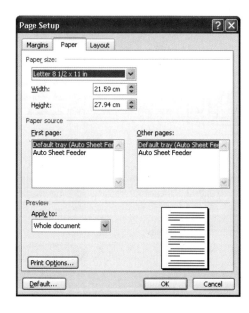

Automatic customization

Sometimes a vast number of menu options and toolbar icons can be a daunting and confusing sight. To simplify and help speed things up, Word's menus and toolbars are self-customizing.

Personalized menus

When you first use Word, its menus display the features which Microsoft believes are used 95% of the time. Features which are infrequently used are not immediately visible. This is demonstrated in the illustrations below.

Automatic customization applies to toolbars as well as menus.

Here are some useful points about toolbars:

- *if possible, they display on a single row*
- *they overlap when there isn't enough room on-screen*
- *icons are "promoted" and "demoted" like menu entries*
- *demoted icons are shown in a separate fly-out, reached by clicking the Toolbar Options button.*

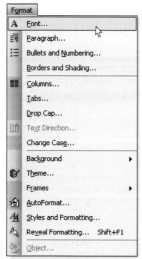

The first time you use Word, opening up the Format menu will show you an abbreviated set of options.

Wait a few seconds, or click the ❯ button to see the full menu.

As you continue to use Word, it will remember which options are the ones you use most often. The menus and toolbars will continuously self-customize, so that their short versions reflect your usage.

Help

Word features two different ways for you to access help.

General help

1 Press the F1 key, or choose Microsoft Word Help from the Help menu.

2 Enter your Help search text here.

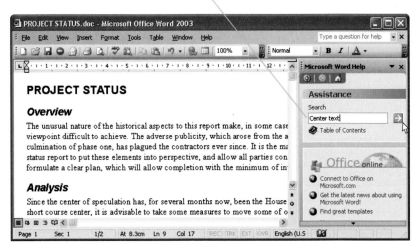

If you are connected to the Internet, Word will communicate with Microsoft.com to access a wide range of continuously updated information. If you want to force Word to use just the help stored locally on your PC, select Offline Help from the Search settings at the bottom of the Task Pane.

3 Click the Start searching button:

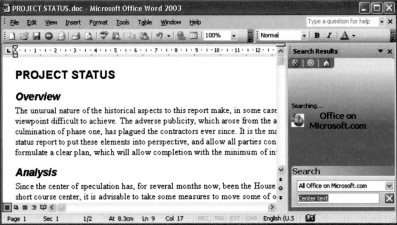

4 The search results are summarized in the Task Pane. Click on any of the blue titles to see the full Help text.

Another way to access Word's Help features is to type a question into the text box labelled "Type a question for help" located at the top right of the screen. After entering your question, pressing the Return key will activate the Help search, with the results displayed in the normal way:

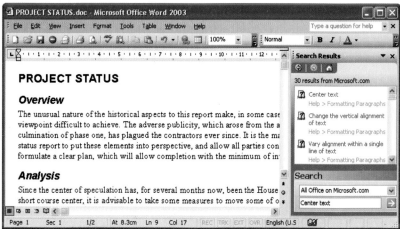

5 The Microsoft Word Help window appears. This may contain hyperlinks to related topics, or full definitions of key terms.

6 The Help window also has icons at the top for Auto Tiling, for moving back and forward through visited pages (just like a web browser), and for printing.

Help Boxes

If you allow your mouse pointer to rest over an icon for a moment, a Help box will appear. This gives you a brief explanation of the icon's function.

Help box

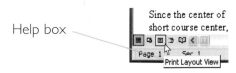

Using Smart Tags

Word recognizes certain types of data and underlines them with a dotted purple underline or a small blue box. When you move the mouse pointer over the line/box an "action button" appears. This provides access to useful commands.

Examples of different Smart Tags

If you are not yet familiar with Cut, Copy and Paste procedures, see Chapter 4 "Working with a document".

Recently pasted text has a Paste Options Smart Tag added to it, allowing you to decide on formatting.

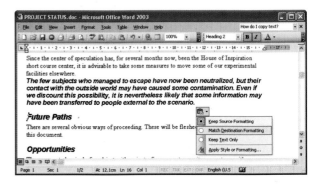

You can disable Smart Tags. In the Tools menu click AutoCorrect Options. In the dialog, select the Smart Tags tab. Uncheck the option "Label text with Smart Tags".

Some text, such as days of the week or the first word of a sentence, is automatically capitalized. This can be overridden using the pop-up menu.

In this example a name is recognized as an online contact.

Types of data to which Word applies Smart Tags include the following:

- *dates/times*
- *places/addresses*
- *Outlook email recipients*

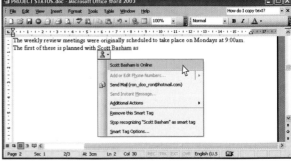

Basic text manipulation

This chapter helps you start entering and manipulating text on the screen. It looks at different ways of editing and formatting type, as well as saving and printing your work.

Covers

The Document window | 20

Click and Type | 24

Multiple text selection | 25

Auto Recover | 25

Handwriting text | 26

The Task Pane | 27

Saving a document | 28

Opening a document | 28

Print Preview | 29

Printing a document | 30

Chapter Two

The Document window

The first skill to practise is inserting new text into a document.

The New Document icon looks like this:

1   If there is no Document window, then create a new one by clicking on the New icon in the top left of the standard toolbar.

2   Enter a sentence of example text.

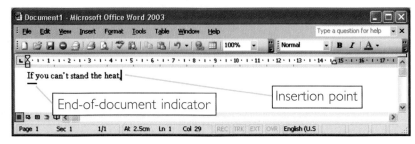

If you can't stand the heat,

End-of-document indicator   Insertion point

Word automatically works out when to take a new line without breaking words. If you want to start a new paragraph, press the Return or Enter key.

The vertical line is your *insertion point*, indicating where new text will appear. You can move the insertion point using the cursor (arrow) keys, or by clicking a new position with the mouse.

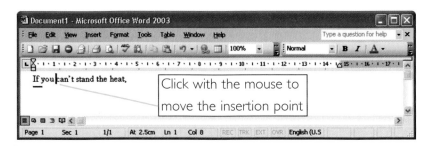

If you can't stand the heat,

Click with the mouse to move the insertion point

When the insertion point is in the correct position type some new text. It will appear at the insertion point.

Note that the words to the right of the insertion point move along to accommodate the text you are inserting.

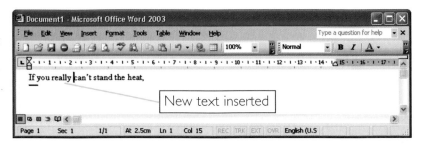

If you really can't stand the heat,

New text inserted

Deleting text with the Backspace key

Place the insertion point just after the text you want to delete.

2 Press the Backspace key once to erase each character to the *left*.

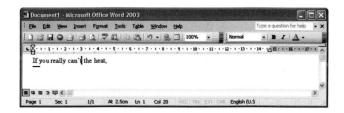

Deleting text with the Delete key

This time, move the insertion point before the text to be deleted.

2 Press the Delete key once to erase each character to the *right*.

Selecting text

Select text by dragging horizontally across it.

By default, Word is in Insert mode. This means that when you add new text, existing text makes room for it. However, Word also has an alternative mode called Overtype. In Overtype mode, new text replaces any text to the right of the insertion point. To enter (or leave) Overtype mode, press the Insert key.

Start dragging here

Finish dragging here

Replacing selected text

Anything you type will replace the currently selected text.

Adding more text to the end of the document

To select all text within a document, press Ctrl+A.

Make sure the insertion point is at the end of the document text.

2 Add the text:

Changing the appearance of text

1   Select the text, open the Size drop-down menu from the toolbar, and increase the point size to around twice the previous value.

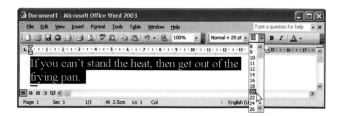

2   Select a single word and use the toolbar to choose Bold.

The keyboard shortcut for Bold is Ctrl+B.

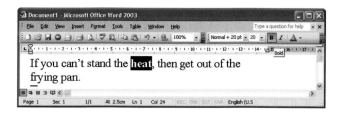

3   To select text over more than one line, drag over the area:

4   To select multiple lines drag down within the left margin.

Note the differently angled pointer

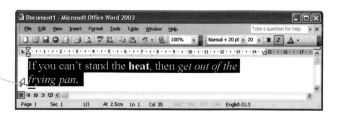

5 Alternatively, you can double-click to select a single word, or triple-click to select an entire paragraph.

6 If you click an insertion point and then type more text, the new text takes its attributes (appearance) from the previous character.

Note that when you are inserting, new text takes on the attributes of the existing character to the left, not the character to the right.

Click and Type

In Print Layout or Web Layout view you can add text virtually anywhere on the page. Double-click to establish an insertion point.

If Click and Type doesn't appear to work, first make sure that you're in Print Layout or Web Layout view. Then open the Tools menu and choose Options. Select the Edit tab and make sure that Click and Type is activated.

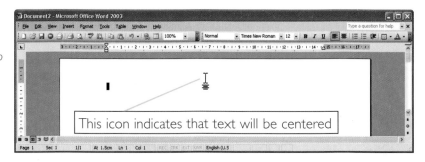

This icon indicates that text will be centered

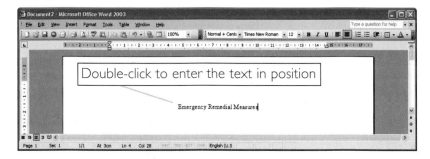

Double-click to enter the text in position

Multiple text selection

It is also possible to select discontinuous blocks of text.

1 Make the first selection in the normal way.

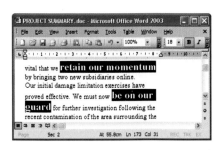

2 Hold down the Control key to select a second block of text without deselecting the first.

3 Repeat this process for any additional blocks of text. You can then apply formatting to everything which has been selected.

Auto Recover

If your PC has problems which cause Word to crash or otherwise terminate unexpectedly, Auto Recovery can often rescue your most recent work.

1 Once your computer is up and running again, restart Word.

2 The Document Recovery options will appear automatically. You may be offered different versions of your document, e.g. the one you last saved, and the one Word recovered.

If you are offered multiple versions don't assume that the recovered or repaired version of your document is always the one you should use. Carefully check both before you decide which is better.

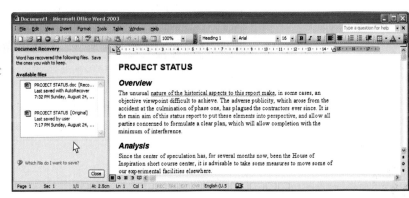

Handwriting text

You can handwrite text into a special writing pad and have Word convert it into standard text. You can also use a virtual keyboard to enter text.

If the language bar (depicted below) is not visible in the Taskbar then go to the Windows Control Panel. Double-click Regional and Language Options and select the Languages tab in the dialog which appears. Under Text Services and Input Languages, click the Details button. Under Preferences, click Language Bar and select the option Show the Language Bar.

1 Click Handwriting on the Language Bar:

2 Select Writing Pad.

3 Handwrite text on the line in the Writing Pad (don't pause between letters but do leave a space after words) – Word enters the text as soon as it recognizes it.

You can import handwritten notes made on a Handheld or Pocket PC into Word – see the device's documentation. Alternatively, you can write using a graphics tablet attached to your PC, or even the mouse.

By default, Word converts handwriting to text. However, you can have it entered as handwriting (which can still be formatted in the normal way). Click this button in the Writing Pad:

The Task Pane

The keyboard shortcut to switch the Task Pane on and off is Ctrl+F1.

The Task Pane is a useful way of manipulating settings without going into a series of dialog boxes. The benefit is that you can try out options and immediately see their effect without having to wait until you have closed down the dialog box.

The Task Pane can be used to show 14 different sets of controls, including Clipboard, Research, Clip Art, Styles and Formatting and Mail Merge facilities.

1   Ensure the Task Pane is active by checking its entry in the View menu.

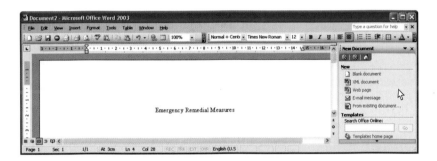

Like toolbars, the Task Pane can be undocked from the main window. To do this, simply drag on its Title bar towards the center of the screen, until the Task Pane becomes "free floating".

2   If the New Document controls are not visible, then select New Document from the drop-down menu in the Task Pane's top right corner.

3   You can now choose to start different types of new document. You can also base a document on a predefined Template. See Chapter 9 "Templates and Wizards" for more information.

4   Other functions of the Task Pane are covered throughout the rest of this book.

Saving a document

1. To save your work either choose Save from the File menu, or click on the Save icon in the toolbar:

2. If necessary, select the correct drive and folder.

3. Enter the file name and click Save.

4. If you have finished with the document, choose Close from the File menu.

Opening a document

Choose Open from the File menu or click on the Open icon:

Note that the last few files used are listed in the lower section of the File menu, and can be selected directly.

Print Preview

Note that the Print Preview icon looks like this:

Before you print a document, you may wish to check it on-screen, in order to eliminate any errors that were not spotted at the basic text-proofing stage. Word offers a facility, Print Preview, which shows you all the pages of your document exactly as they will print, with none of the modifications made by the normal Word views. To access this special view, select Print Preview from the File menu, or select the corresponding icon from the toolbar.

The following screen appears:

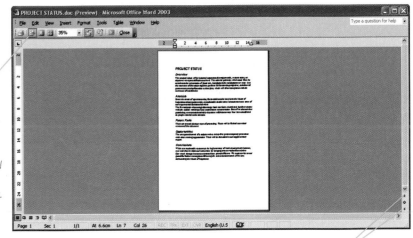

Click here to edit the text in Print Preview (the cursor changes back to its normal text-editing shape). Then click in the text and make your changes.

Click on these buttons to move through the pages of your document.

Note that the cursor is initially in the shape of a magnifying glass. To zoom in to a particular area of the page, click over it with the left mouse button; to zoom out, click a second time.

If you are satisfied with your document, select Print from the File menu, or click the Print icon: 🖨 (see Page 30). If you want to continue editing, click Close instead.

Printing a document

1 Choose Print from the File menu to see the following dialog:

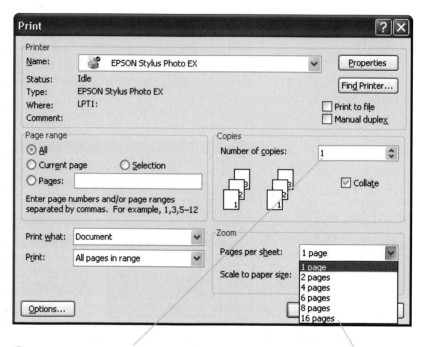

2 Enter the number of copies required.

3 Click OK to go ahead, or Cancel to abort.

You can use the Zoom facility to print out small versions of pages, up to sixteen on a single sheet

The method detailed above allows you the greatest control over how your document is printed. If, however, you do not need to make any refinements to the printing method, there is a much quicker way to print: simply click the Print icon in the Toolbar:

This begins to print immediately, bypassing the Print dialog box and using the default print settings.

Formatting text

This chapter looks at ways in which you can change the appearance of your text. You'll start by examining what you can change on a character level. Then you'll see what you can control on a paragraph-by-paragraph basis.

Covers

Character-level formatting | 32

The Font dialog box | 34

Paragraph-level formatting | 36

Forms of alignment | 36

Bulleted paragraphs | 37

Advanced bulleting | 38

Numbered paragraphs | 40

Advanced numbering | 41

Outline numbered lists | 42

Formatting with the Task pane | 43

The Paragraph dialog box | 44

Chapter Three

Character-level formatting

What does "character-level" mean?

Character-level attributes include font name, size, emboldening, underlining and all sorts of other effects which can be applied to individual characters. If required, every single character could be given different attributes (although this would tend to make your document look a little like a ransom letter).

Using the Formatting toolbar

If you highlight a portion of text, the toolbar will automatically indicate its current formatting options.

1 Select the text which you want to format.

2 Choose the font required from the toolbar drop-down menu:

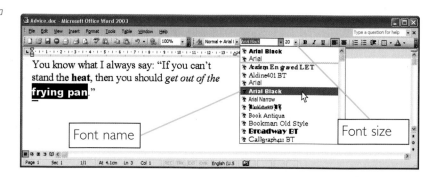

A font is a collection of characters with a particular visual style. Common fonts include:

Times or Times New Roman (useful for main text)

Arial (useful for headings)

Courier (the typewriter font)

3 Look at the font names in the drop-down list:

Printer icon

The most recently
used fonts appear
above this line.

TrueType symbol

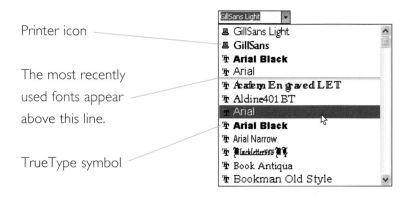

- A printer icon beside the name indicates a printer font. Your machine will use the closest available screen font (which may not match the printed output exactly).

- A double T symbol indicates a TrueType font, which is used for both screen display and printing.

- No symbol beside the font name means that it is a screen font. Check your printer can reproduce this to a high enough quality.

4 You can use the toolbar buttons for effects such as Bold or Italic.

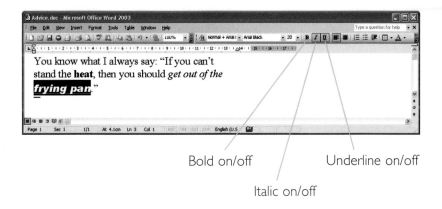

Bold on/off

Italic on/off

Underline on/off

The Font dialog box

This controls all aspects of character-level formatting.

1 Select the text to change.

2 Either choose Font from the Format menu, then go to Step 4, or click your right mouse button inside the document window.

Right-clicking brings up a menu that contains options which are relevant to the task in hand. Later you will see that it changes depending on your current context.

To quickly change the font, press Ctrl+Shift+F then type the first few letters of the Font name. Look at the Formatting toolbar to see the name of the font selected.

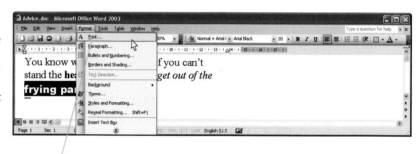

3 Choose Font.

4 This dialog box appears. Experiment with the different options, noting how they affect the Preview image.

5 Click on the Character Spacing tab.

Kerning is a process used to adjust the space between certain combinations of characters. For example, when the letters "T" and "o" occur next to each other, normal spacing appears to be too wide. Kerning brings these together to create the illusion of normal spacing. Since kerning slows down the screen redraw you can either switch it off altogether or activate it only for larger font sizes (where space is more noticeable).

6 Click on the Text Effects tab.

7 This feature allows you to enhance text by adding animated effects to it.

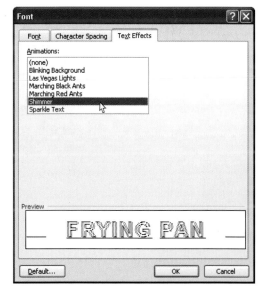

Paragraph-level formatting

Remember that a heading is often a single-line paragraph.

What does "paragraph-level" mean?

Options like alignment, indents and space above/below refer to whole paragraphs (each has only one set of these attributes).

Formatting with the Toolbar

If you are changing just one paragraph you need only click an insertion point somewhere within it. Any change to a paragraph-level attribute will always affect the entire paragraph surrounding the insertion point.

| 1 | Select the paragraph(s) to format.

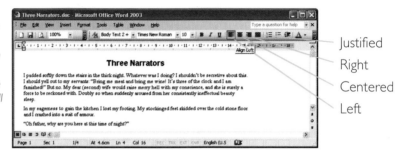

Justified
Right
Centered
Left

2 Click one of the alignment icons in the formatting toolbar.

Forms of alignment

If you use left, right or center alignment, text lines up along its left edge, right edge and halfway between (centered), respectively.

If you justify your text, then spacing is adjusted so that each line within a paragraph begins and ends in the same position (dictated by the margins and indents) giving a regular appearance. Below is an example of justified text:

The last line of every justified paragraph is only aligned left, allowing the reader to easily distinguish one paragraph from another.

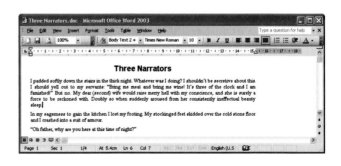

Bulleted paragraphs

Activating Bullets

1 Select the paragraphs to be bulleted.

2 Click on the Bullets icon in the Formatting toolbar.

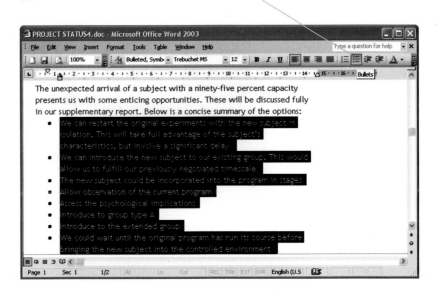

Removing Bullets

1 If necessary, re-select the bulleted paragraphs.

2 Click on the Bullets icon a second time.

Automatic Bullets

This is similar to the automatic numbering feature discussed on Page 40. If you begin a paragraph with an asterisk, enter text in the normal way, and then press Return, Word automatically replaces the asterisk with a bullet, and starts the next paragraph with another. When you reach the end of the list that you want bulleted, erase the bullet that has just been created.

Advanced bulleting

1 Select the text to be bulleted.

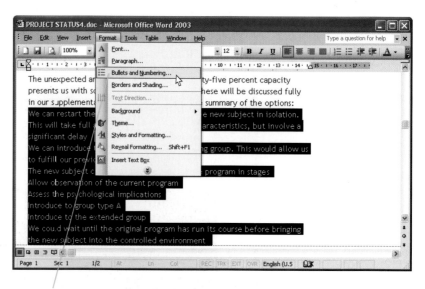

2 Choose Bullets and Numbering from the Format menu.

You can also select Bullets and Numbering from the menu which appears when you click in the document window with the right mouse button.

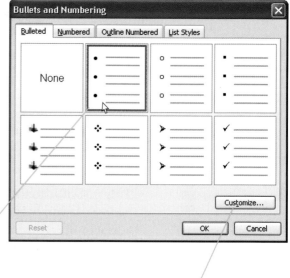

3 Choose the type of bullet.

4 Click on Customize to see further options.

If you click on the Picture button in this dialog box you'll be able to select from a range of graphic bullets, or even import a custom graphic from a file.

5 Choose the required settings. Click on the required bullet...

6 ...or click here to select another from the complete range of characters.

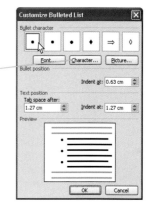

7 Select the font and character.

8 Click OK to exit all dialogs.

The selected text is now bulleted:

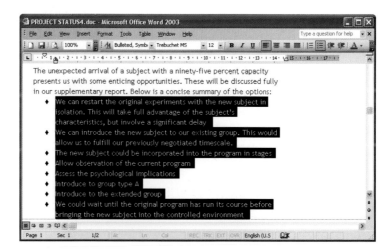

Numbered paragraphs

1   Select the paragraphs to be numbered.

2   Click on the Numbering icon in the Formatting toolbar.

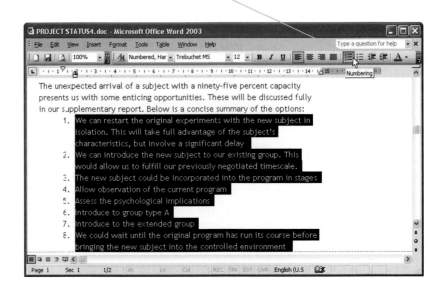

Removing numbers

1   If necessary, re-select the numbered paragraphs.

2   Click on the Numbering icon a second time.

Automatic numbering

If you begin a paragraph with a number, enter text in the normal way, and then press Return, Word automatically starts the next paragraph with the next number. When you reach the end of the list that you want numbered, simply erase the number that has just been created.

Advanced numbering

1. Select the text to be numbered.

2. Right-click the selected text. Choose Bullets and Numbering from the drop-down menu.

3. Select the Numbered tab.

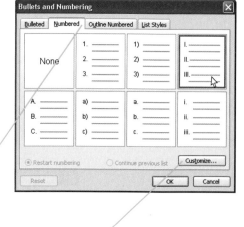

4. Choose a style or click on Customize.

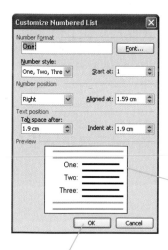

5. Experiment with different settings, referring to the Preview box.

6. Click OK

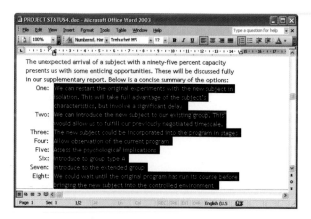

Outline numbered lists

Outline numbered lists contain nested sets of headings and subheadings. Because this function helps you to structure your numbered lists, you are likely to use it differently to the normal numbering function discussed on Page 41.

1   With the cursor positioned at the point where you want to begin your multi-level structured list, select Bullets and Numbering from the Format menu, and choose the Outline Numbered tab.

2   Select a number style from the top row (i.e. those that don't contain any heading styles).

3   Click OK.

4   Back in the Word document enter your list, pressing Return at the end of each element (see the Hot Tip in the margin).

To place a line at a subordinate level to the one above it, right-click anywhere in the line, and select Increase Indent. To move a line to a higher level, select Decrease Indent.

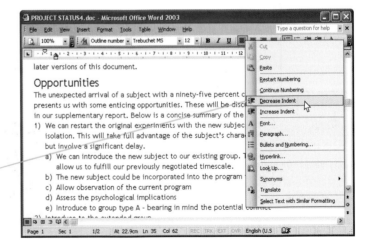

Formatting with the Task pane

The Task Pane lets you control text formatting without having to open up dialog boxes.

DON'T FORGET

Using the Task Pane means that you can experiment with settings much more interactively, as you'll immediately see the result of any changes.

First make sure that the Task Pane can be seen. To switch it on, choose Task Pane from the View menu.

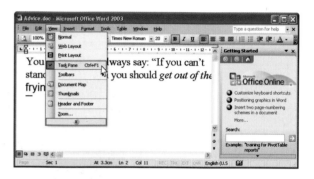

HOT TIP

The keyboard shortcut to show or hide the Task Pane is Ctrl+F1.

Click here to open the drop-down menu then select Styles and Formatting.

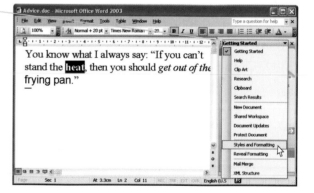

DON'T FORGET

The Task Pane can be hidden, moved, docked and undocked just like any other toolbar (see Chapter 1 "Getting to know Word").

HOT TIP

You can also apply and modify Styles using the Task Pane. See Chapter 5 "Styles and Themes" for more about this.

The Task Pane displays current text settings, which you can modify.

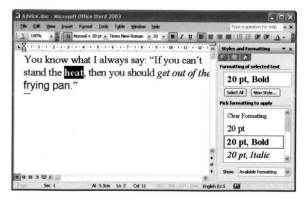

The Paragraph dialog box

This controls all aspects of paragraph-level formatting.

1 Select the text to be formatted.

2 Either choose Paragraph from the Format menu, or...

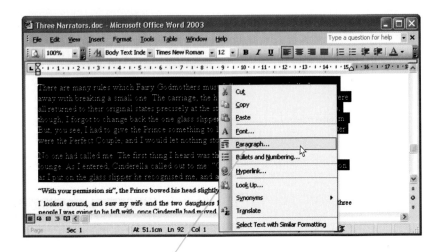

3 ...click your right mouse button somewhere within the document window and select Paragraph from the pop-up menu.

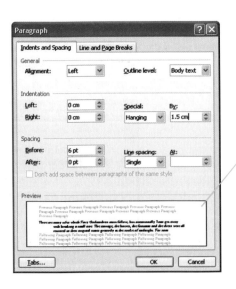

4 Experiment with the different paragraph controls, checking the results in the Preview image. You can adjust the left and right indent, the space above and below a paragraph, or the line spacing within a paragraph.

In the example below, a (vertical) space before of 6 points and a special hanging indent of 1.5 cm have been set:

Hanging indents keep the first line of each paragraph exactly at the left margin, while moving all subsequent lines to the right by a fixed distance.

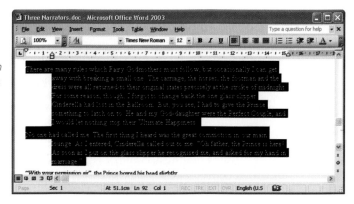

In the following example, line spacing has been changed to exactly 16 points. This means each line in the selected paragraphs will be given exactly 16 points of vertical space regardless of the font size.

72 points are approximately equal to 1 inch. 12 points are equal to the size of normal typewriter text.

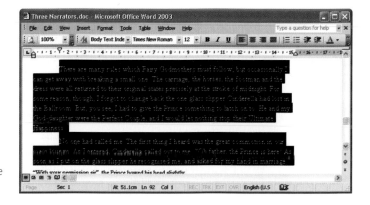

It is often useful to adjust vertical spacing using points, so that the space between paragraphs uses the same measuring system as the paragraphs themselves.

The Points system of measurement

This system was introduced in the USA in the nineteenth century and then adopted by the UK and some European countries.

It provides a standard way of measuring the size of type, and often refers to the vertical dimension of characters in a given font.

The Line and Page Breaks Tab

1 Activate the Paragraph dialog box (either from the Format menu or by clicking in the document window with the right mouse button).

A widow is a single line of text at the beginning of a paragraph separated from the rest by a page break. An orphan is a similar line at the end of a paragraph. Both widows and orphans look unattractive and should be avoided if possible.

2 Choose the Line and Page Breaks tab.

3 Apply any of these settings — see below.

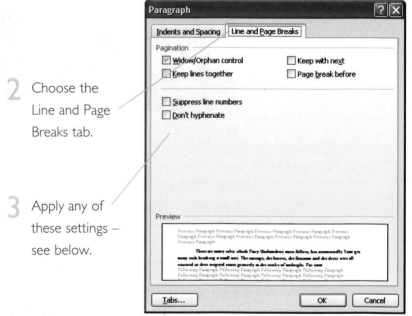

Widow/Orphan control
This option instructs Word to automatically move text onto the next page if necessary to avoid widows and orphans.

Keep lines together
Word will move the text so that the paragraph is not broken over two pages.

Keep with next
Makes sure that the text is kept with the following paragraph, and not broken over two pages.

Page break before
Forces a new page at the start of the paragraph.

Suppress line numbers
Switches off numbering for this paragraph if line numbers have been used, renumbering the surrounding paragraphs if necessary.

Don't hyphenate
Deactivates hyphenation.

Working with a document

This chapter helps you to find your way around a document, looking at scrolling, selecting different views and zooming in and out of the page. Additionally you'll look at Cut, Copy and Paste, the Format Painter tool and several other helpful document-formatting features.

Covers

Scrolling | 48

Zooming | 49

The Ruler | 50

Cut and Paste | 50

Copy and Paste | 52

The Task Pane Clipboard | 53

Undo and Redo | 54

Page breaks | 55

Defining sections | 55

Using columns with sections | 56

Headers and footers | 58

The Format Painter | 60

Document properties | 61

The Document Map | 62

Chapter Four

Scrolling

When your text is too large for the document window, you'll need to use one of the following navigation methods:

The scroll boxes let you know where you are in a document. For example, when the vertical scroll box is right at the top of the scroll bar, you are looking at the top (the beginning) of the document.

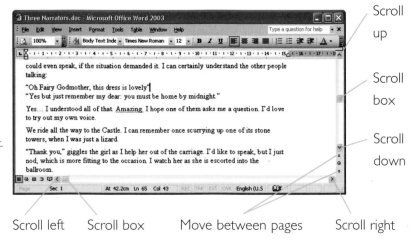

Scroll up

Scroll box

Scroll down

Scroll left   Scroll box   Move between pages   Scroll right

As you scroll down, the scroll box moves down like a lift through a lift shaft. The size of the box indicates how much of the document you are currently viewing. For example, if the box is one third the size of the scroll bar, then you're viewing a third of the document.

Quick ways to scroll

- Drag the scroll box directly to a new position.

- Click in the scroll bar to either side of the scroll box. The document will scroll in that direction one screen at a time.

- As you move your insertion point, Word will scroll automatically so that it can always be seen.

The Page Up and Page Down keys will scroll you up and down one screen at a time.

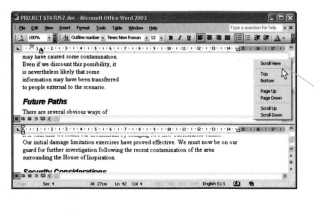

If you right-click in a scrollbar, this menu gives you another quick way to move through the document.

Zooming

You can use the Zoom drop-down menu to control the level of magnification used by the document window.

The Page Width option automatically zooms in or out so that the entire width of the page is displayed.

Drop-down
Zoom menu

HOT TIP

If you can afford the space on screen, always maximize both the document window and the Word window itself by clicking on the Maximize button.

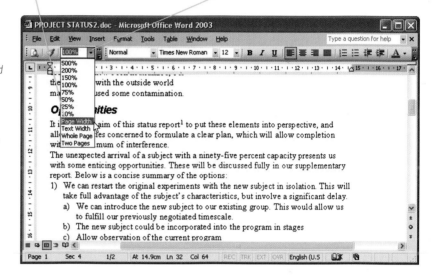

In Print Layout view you can display more than one page at a time.

Remember that the more you magnify the page, the more you'll need to scroll. Always try to view the entire horizontal line of text, since frequent horizontal scrolling can be tedious.

Resizing windows

To allocate the greatest possible amount of space to a window, click on the Maximize button. To restore it to its non-maximized size, click on the Restore button.

DON'T FORGET

If the Restore symbol is visible, this indicates that your current window is already maximized. If you click on it, the window will restore to its non-maximized size.

Maximize button   Restore button

These are located in a window's top right-hand corner. To adjust the dimensions of a non-maximized window, rest the cursor over one of the window's edges (the cursor changes to a double-headed arrow), then drag the edge to where you want it.

The Ruler

The Ruler shows the tabs and indents used for any selected text.

You can also access these controls numerically from the Paragraph dialog box. See Chapter 3 "Formatting text".

| If the Ruler is not visible, choose Ruler from the View menu.

2 Select one or more paragraphs. Try moving the indent markers:

General left indent   First-line indent   Default tab stops

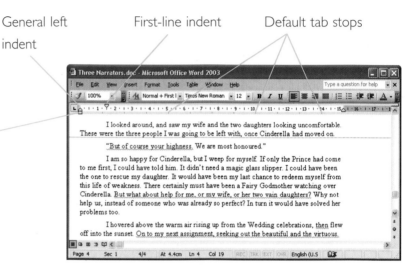

There is a small square block directly below the left indent marker. Dragging this will move both the left and first line indent markers together.

Cut and Paste

| Select the text to be moved.

2 Right-click on the selected text, then choose Cut.

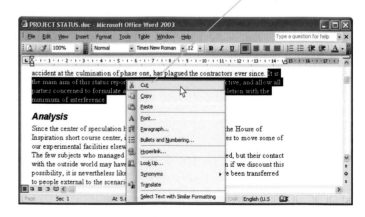

You can also Cut and Paste using the Edit menu, or the keyboard shortcuts Ctrl+X, Ctrl+V respectively.

The text is removed and put into the Clipboard.

3 At the destination click the right mouse button and choose Paste.

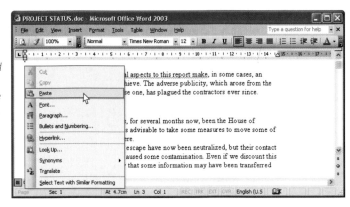

You can also use the Cut, Copy and Paste buttons (see below) in the Standard Toolbar.

Cut

Copy

Paste

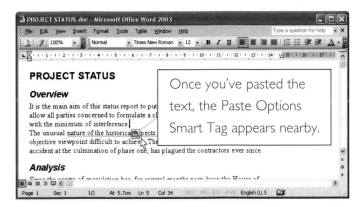

Once you've pasted the text, the Paste Options Smart Tag appears nearby.

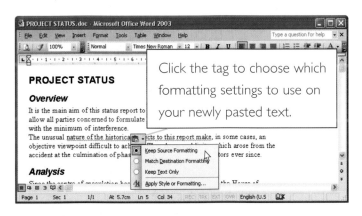

Click the tag to choose which formatting settings to use on your newly pasted text.

Copy and Paste

You can also Copy and Paste using the Edit menu, or the keyboard shortcuts Ctrl+C, Ctrl+V.

1 Select the text to be copied.

2 Right-click on the selected text, then choose Copy.

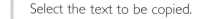

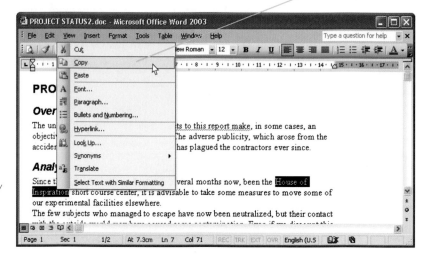

The quickest way to move text is to select it, then drag (from anywhere within the selected area) directly to the new position.

The text is copied into the Clipboard.

3 Position the insertion point at the destination. Click the right mouse button, then choose Paste. Once something is in the Clipboard, you can paste it as many times as you like.

If you drag the selected area with the Control key held down, the text will be copied to the new position.

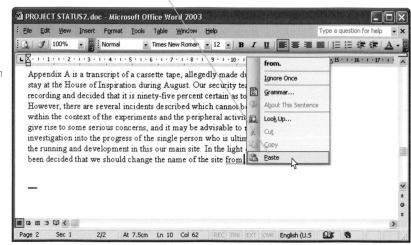

The Task Pane Clipboard

The Task Pane has a Clipboard section offering additional features.

1 Make sure the Task Pane is visible (if not, activate it from the View menu). Open its drop-down menu and select Clipboard.

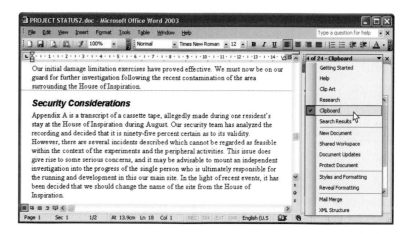

2 Each time you choose Copy, an extra item appears in the Clipboard area. If you click directly on the item in the Clipboard, a drop-down menu allows you to delete or paste the item.

Note that buttons near the top of the Clipboard area allow you to Paste All or Clear All items in the Clipboard.

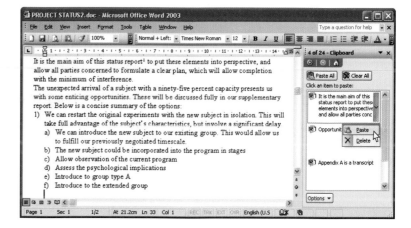

The Options button lets you place an icon for the Clipboard in the Windows System Tray, which may be useful if you are copying and pasting between different Clipboard-compatible applications.

Undo and Redo

1 Use the Undo button or Ctrl+Z to undo the last action.

2 Alternatively, open the Undo menu to undo more actions.

When undoing or redoing actions using the drop-down menus, drag the cursor down until the actions that you want to undo or redo are highlighted, then release the mouse button.

Undo button   Undo drop-down menu button

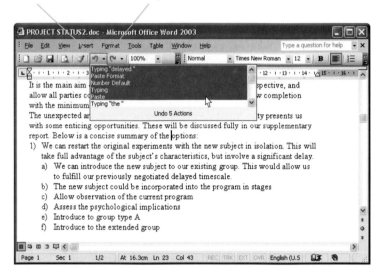

3 To redo the undone actions, type Ctr+Y or use the Redo menu.

Redo button   Redo drop-down menu button

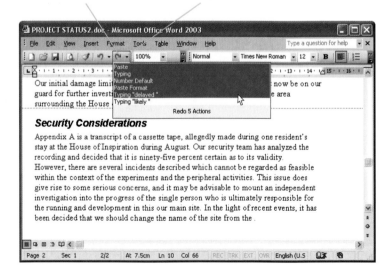

Page breaks

The keyboard shortcut for page break is Ctrl+Return.
To delete a page break, simply select it by clicking in the left margin area then pressing Delete.

Word automatically calculates the position of page breaks. These appear in the document window as a dotted horizontal line (a "soft" page break). However, you can force page breaks, as follows:

1 Choose Break... from the Insert menu.

2 Make sure that Page break is selected.

A "hard" page break is inserted.

Defining sections

Sections can be used to help organize your document. They also allow you to vary its layout, even within a single page.

1 Click an insertion point part of the way through your document (between paragraphs).

2 Make sure that Page break is selected.

3 Under Section break types choose Continuous. Click OK.

The document is now divided into two sections. In Normal View, you can see the section break as a horizontal dotted line.

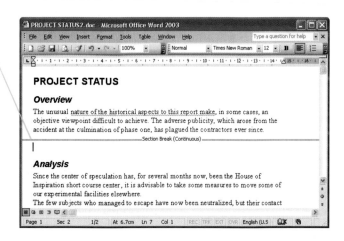

Using columns with sections

1 Make sure you are using a document which has been divided into two or more sections.

2 Click the insertion point somewhere in the second section, then choose Columns from the Format menu.

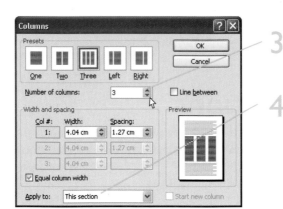

3 Set the number of columns.

4 From the Apply to drop-down menu, make sure that the columns are applied only to This section.

5 Click OK.

You now have a mixed column layout:

Print Layout view is ideal if you want to see your text arranged in columns.

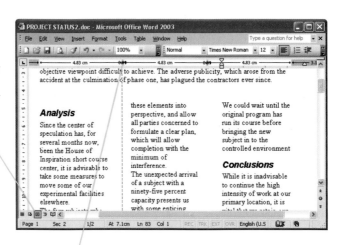

If you drag with the Alt key held down, Word will display the horizontal measurements in the ruler.

6 You can also adjust the width of columns by dragging their boundary markers in the ruler.

Column breaks

You can force text to start in a new column by adding a hard break.

1 Place the insertion point and choose Break from the Insert menu.

2 Select the Column break radio button, then click OK.

This will force the text after the insertion point into a new column.

Balancing columns

If there is enough space on the page to accommodate all of your column text, you can balance the columns neatly:

1 Click the insertion point at the end of the last column and choose Break from the Insert menu.

2 Insert a Continuous section break. The columns will be balanced to within a line or two of each other.

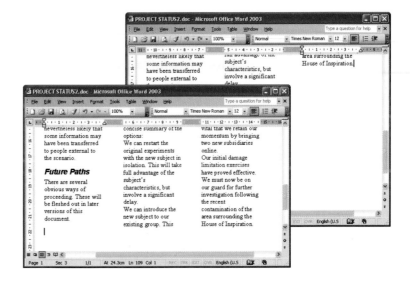

Headers and footers

Headers normally appear at the top of every page, footers at the bottom (an example being "Word 2003 in easy steps" on this page).

Creating/modifying a header

1 Choose Header and Footer from the View menu.

Word will automatically change to Print Layout View. The main page text will be grayed out to let you concentrate on the header. The Header and Footer toolbar will also appear.

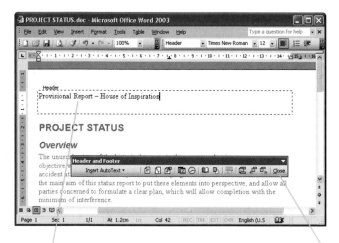

2 Enter the text and apply formatting as required.

3 Click Close when you're finished.

The Header and Footer Toolbar

Use this palette also to insert AutoText. To learn more about AutoText see Chapter 8 "Automatic features".

Insert # of pages   Insert date   Insert time   Switch between header and footer   Show previous/next

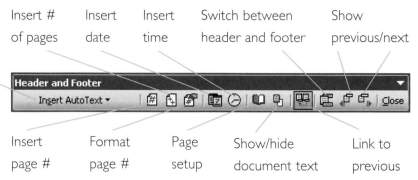

Insert page #   Format page #   Page setup   Show/hide document text   Link to previous

Creating/modifying a footer

1 Click on the Switch Between Header and Footer button in the toolbar. This will take you to the footer text.

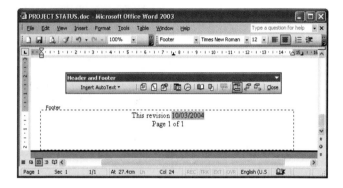

2 Enter the footer text. You can include automatic page numbers, or the current date or time by clicking on the relevant button in the toolbar.

3 Click Close when you're finished.

Now the header and footer text is grayed out, and you can edit the main text again. Note that the picture below shows Print Layout view. In Normal view, headers and footers do not appear at all.

By default, the header and footer on a page will apply to all remaining pages in the document. You can override this by editing the headers/footers for other pages separately.

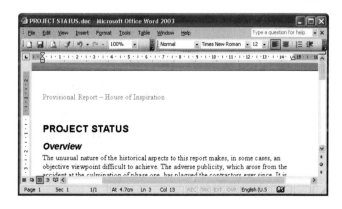

The Format Painter

This allows you to copy the formatting options from one piece of text to another.

Select the source text and click on the Format Painter icon.

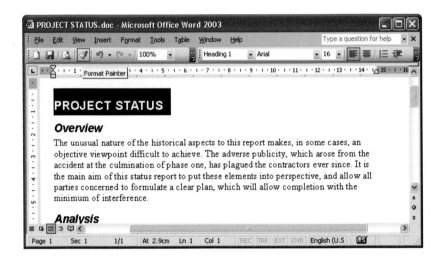

Now drag across the destination text. The formatting is applied to the new text.

To copy formatting to more than one destination, simply double-click the Format Painter icon. You can then apply the new formatting to as many pieces of text as you wish. When you've finished, either click back on the icon or press the Escape key.

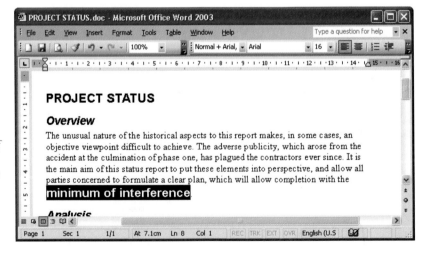

Document properties

Recent versions of Windows introduced file names which could be longer (and so more descriptive) than the Spartan eight characters allowed by MS-DOS. Even so, it is useful to record additional information as part of each Word document, to help you organize your work, and remember your document's purpose.

1 Go to the File menu and choose Properties.

2 Enter the relevant details. These will be saved along with your document.

3 Click OK when you're done.

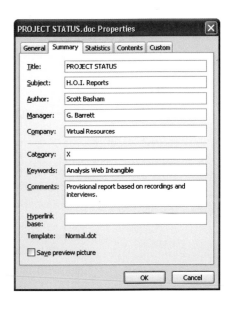

The Statistics tab in the Properties dialog will show you useful information about your document, including the revision number and the total editing time.

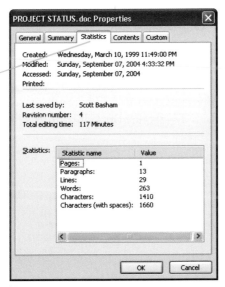

4 When you use the Open document dialog, you can click on the Advanced button to tell Word to search on the basis of the information entered in a document's properties.

The Document Map

The Document Map is a feature which uses the headings in your document to create an outline of the document's structure. It appears in a separate pane to the left of the main editing area, and can be used to navigate easily through the document. To display the Document Map, do the following:

Click on the Document Map button.

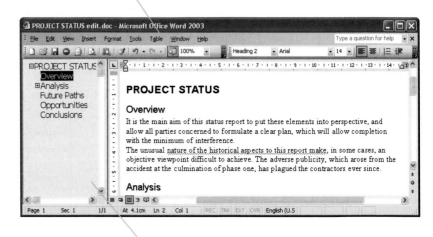

The Document Map frame

To jump to a heading listed in the Document Map, simply click on its entry.

Note that, in the illustration above, the heading Analysis has a small plus sign next to it. This indicates that there are subheadings beneath it. To display these headings, click on the plus sign:

To collapse the structure to show only the main headings, click on the minus sign.

The subheadings are now displayed.

Styles and Themes

Styles help you to easily apply a consistent set of formatting commands to main text, headings and other elements of your document. Once you start using styles, you'll be able to control your document's presentation with the minimum of tedious manual editing.

Themes allow you to give a collection of your documents the same consistent look and feel.

Covers

Using the default Styles | 64

Editing an existing Style | 65

Creating a new Style | 66

The Style dialog box | 67

Character-level Styles | 69

AutoFormat | 70

Themes | 71

The Style Gallery | 72

Displaying Style names | 74

Chapter Five

Using the default Styles

A Style is a complete collection of type attributes saved under a single name. There are two main benefits to this:

- Your document will have a visual consistency if, for example, all your subheadings look the same.

- You can quickly make drastic but coherent changes to the format of your document by redefining the Styles already used by the text.

Applying a Style

1. Select the text.

2. Select a Style from the drop-down menu:

You can also apply a Style using the keyboard shortcut Ctrl+Shift+S.
Then type the first few letters of the style, and select the style from the list.

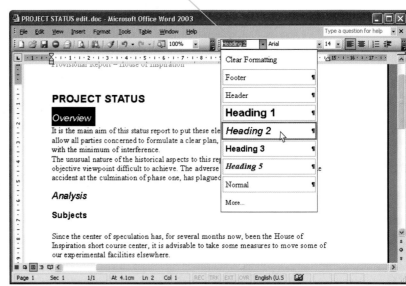

The text has now been set to this Style. Whenever you select text on the page, the drop-down menu will indicate which Style is currently being used.

By default all text starts off using the Normal Style.

Editing an existing Style

1 Make sure the Task Pane is visible. If not, activate it using the View menu. Use its drop-down menu to select the Styles and Formatting controls.

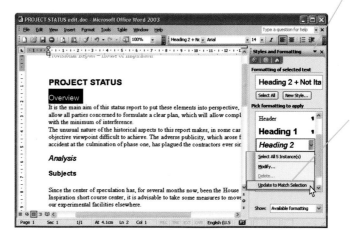

Click here to update the Style

2 Select some text which already uses the Style to be changed.

3 Change the attributes in the normal way, then click on the Style's drop-down menu and choose Update to Match Selection.

All text in the document using this Style will now change automatically.

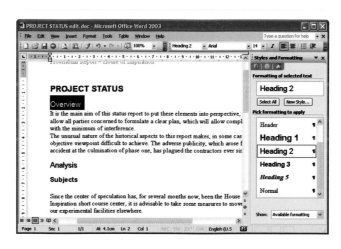

Creating a new Style

You can easily create a new Style by altering existing text and then entering a name for the new Style, which will take these properties.

1 Make sure the Task Pane is visible and displaying its Styles and Formatting controls.

2 Format the text as normal in the document (see Chapter 3 "Formatting text"), then select it.

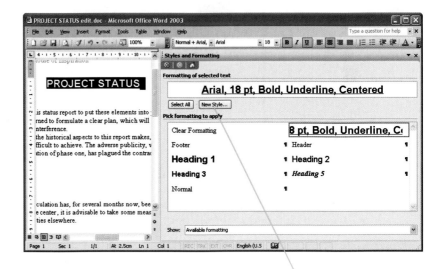

3 When you are happy with its appearance, click on the New Style button in the Task Pane. In the dialog box which appears, enter a name for your Style, then click OK.

You can select this option to Automatically update the Style. If set, then changing the formatting on any text already using the Style will cause the Style's definition to update right away.

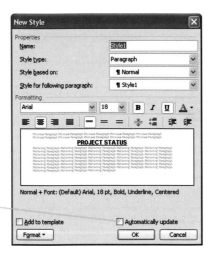

4 The new Style is created, and can now be applied to other text.

The Style dialog box

Word allows you to make most changes from the Formatting toolbar; but the Style dialog allows you to preview potential style changes on a large portion of text, and then (if you change your mind) to cancel out of the dialog without actually making any of the changes. To open the dialog, do the following:

Remember to make sure that the Task Pane is visible and set to display its Styles and Formatting controls.

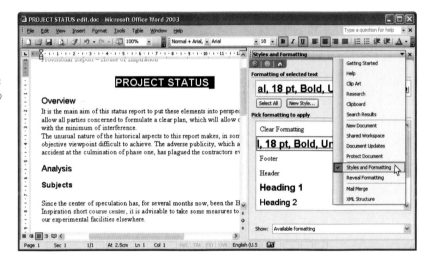

Creating a new Style using the Style dialog box

If the Task Pane is not visible then a quick way to get to the Styles settings is to choose Styles and Formatting from the Format menu. This will both open the Task Pane and switch to the Styles and Formatting controls.

1 Click on the New Style button in the Task Pane.

2 Enter the new Style's name.

3 Use the Format button to fully define the Style. The following pages explain this process in more detail.

4 When you click OK the new Style will be created.

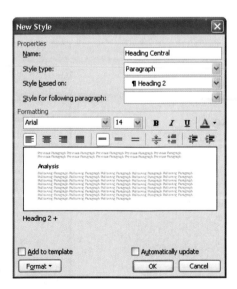

Setting the format

Click on the Format button in the New Style dialog box.

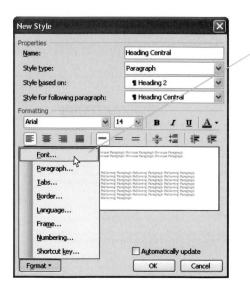

2 This menu appears. Select the dialogs that control the various properties of the Style. Make the appropriate changes, referring to the formatting topics in Chapters 2, 3, and 4.

3 When you have made your changes, click OK. The new Style is added to the list.

Modifying a Style

Select Modify from the menu next to the Style in the Task Pane.

The Modify option takes you to the Modify Style dialog, which functions in the same way as the New Style dialog.

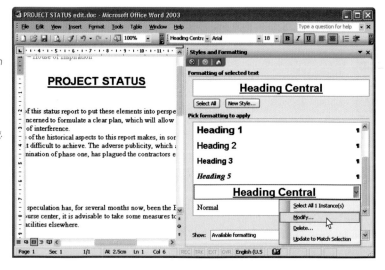

Character-level Styles

Normally Styles only apply to whole paragraphs. If you want to use Styles to control characters without affecting whole paragraphs, you should work with character-level Styles.

Creating a Character-level Style

1 Choose New Style from the Task Pane.

2 Enter a name for the new Style in the usual way.

3 Select Character from the Style type drop-down menu.

4 Use the Format drop-down to set the character-level attributes.

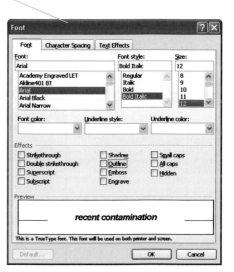

You can now apply your character Style to individual words or phrases without affecting the entire surrounding paragraph.

If text already uses a paragraph Style, then the character Style will override these settings.

Character-level Style names are labelled in the drop-down list with "**a**".
Paragraph Styles are labelled with "¶".

Once a Style has been created, it cannot be changed from a character to a paragraph style or vice versa. However, you can always create a new copy of the Style by choosing New Style from the Task Pane, selecting the Style you want to copy and then clicking on New. Since this is a new Style you can now select the Style type.

AutoFormat

Word uses a feature called AutoFormat to apply suitable Styles automatically to the different parts of your document, without you having to select them. For example, it analyzes whether a paragraph seems to be functioning as body text, as a heading, or as part of a list. You can control AutoFormat settings from the Tools menu.

1 Choose AutoCorrect Options from the Tools menu, then select the AutoFormat As You Type tab.

2 Select which formatting changes AutoFormat should make automatically as you enter your text.

3 Click OK.

These options will now affect any new text entered into your documents.

If you click the Options button, you will be presented with the AutoFormat Options tab, which will allow you to control the types of changes that Word will make.

If AutoFormat was deactivated while you typed in a document, and you subsequently want to have the document formatted automatically, do the following:

1 Select AutoFormat from the Format menu.

2 Tell Word what sort of document this is, then click OK.

Themes

Themes allow you to provide a unified look and feel to a document. They contain settings for styles, bullets, color and graphics.

Applying a Theme to a document

1 Choose Theme from the Format menu. The following dialog box appears:

2 Select a Theme.

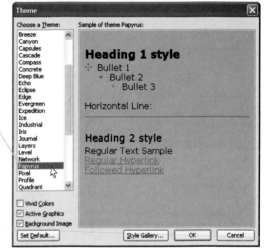

3 Check the Theme sample. If you are happy with its look, click OK.

Your document will now reflect the new Theme.

You can still change your mind at this point by using the Undo button.
Alternatively select a different theme from the Theme dialog box.

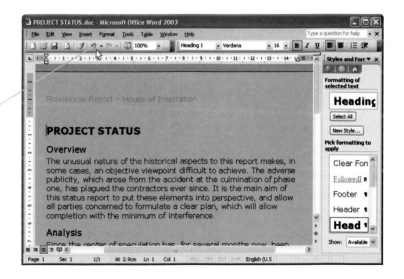

The Style Gallery

When you work on a document, a template is used to tell Word which formatting properties to use for the different character and paragraph Styles. You can use the Style Gallery to apply the properties of different templates, to produce an instant overall change to the appearance of your document.

A template differs from a Theme in that it only contains Style definitions, and no color schemes or graphics. However, a template will generally contain far more Style definitions than a Theme.

1 Go to the Format menu, and choose Theme.

2 Click on the Style Gallery button.

3 Choose a template design then a Preview option. Document previews your document, Example uses its own sample text.

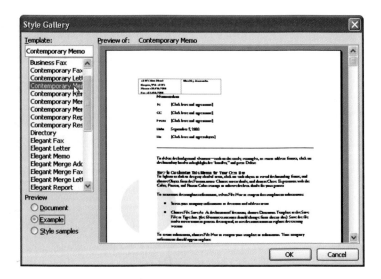

Style samples lists each Style name using its own attributes.

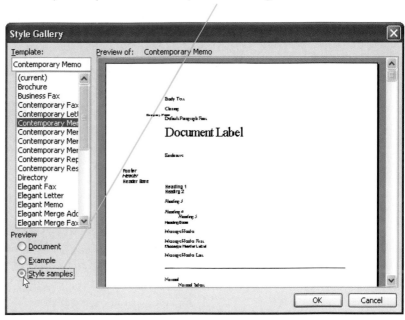

4 Click OK to adopt these new Style definitions in your document.

Your document will now use the Styles from the template.

If your document currently doesn't use any of the Style names defined in the template, then applying the template will have no initial visible effect. However, you can now use these new Styles by applying them manually to your text.

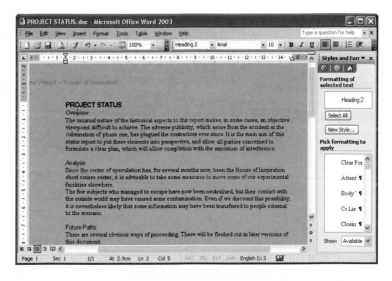

Displaying Style names

Sometimes it's useful to see instantly which Styles are being used by the paragraphs in your document.

1 Make sure that Normal view is active (you can set this using the View menu or the icon at the bottom left of the screen).

2 Choose Options from the Tools menu.

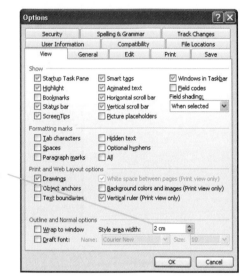

3 Click on the View tab.

4 Set the Style area width to a figure greater than zero.

This example uses a 2cm margin area for listing the Styles used.

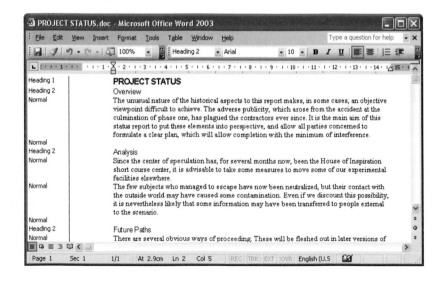

Using Speech Recognition

You can dictate into Word and have your dictation transformed into on-screen text. When errors occur, you can correct them using the mouse and keyboard (in the usual way) or by dictating the replacement. You can also launch menus, toolbar buttons and dialogs with dedicated voice commands.

Covers

Preparing to use Speech Recognition | 76

Dictating text | 77

Entering Voice Commands | 78

Correcting errors | 78

Chapter Six

Preparing to use Speech Recognition

You can dictate text directly into Word. You can also make selections in menus, toolbars, dialogs and the Task Pane.

If you cannot locate the Language bar, open the Windows Control Panel. From Regional and Language Options choose the Languages tab and click the Details button. Under the Preferences heading click the Language Bar button and switch on the option Show the Language bar on the desktop.

Installing/running Speech Recognition

If you haven't installed speech recognition via a custom install, pull down the Tools menu and click Speech.

Preparing Speech Recognition

Before you can dictate into Word, you have to adjust your microphone and carry out a brief 'training' procedure to acclimatize Word to the sound of your voice:

1 Pull down the Tools menu and click Speech.

2 Click Next to begin the training process.

You'll only see the Microphone Wizard the first time you choose Speech from the Tools menu. After this, the Speech option takes you straight into Speech Recognition.

3 Adjust your microphone in line with the instructions then click Next.

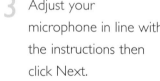

Your use of Speech Recognition will benefit from repeated training. Click the Tools button on the Language Bar and select Training to run through the training Wizard another time.

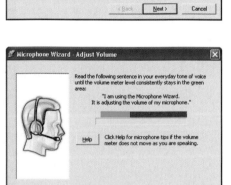

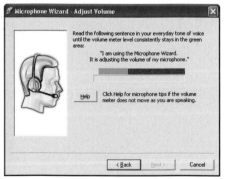

4 Read out the sentence shown then click Next. Complete the rest of the wizard.

Dictating text

If you are not careful in how you set up Speech Recognition, the results may well be poor. Make sure that you use a quality microphone and run through the training procedure enough times for the system to become accustomed to your speech.

1 Follow the procedure on the previous page to prepare speech.

2 If the Microphone option is not already on, click here.

3 The Language bar expands. Click the Dictation button.

For best results keep your environment as quiet as possible, and keep the microphone in the same position relative to your mouth. Pronounce words clearly but don't pause during a word. You'll notice a marked improvement in recognition accuracy after a little practise with the system.

4 Begin dictating. Initially, Word inserts a blue bar on the screen – the text appears as soon as it's recognized.

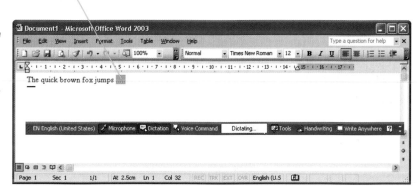

Although impressive, Speech Recognition is not yet advanced enough for you to expect to be able to use Word efficiently using your voice as the only input. For the best results use speech in conjunction with the keyboard and mouse.

5 To close Speech Recognition, choose Speech from the Tools menu.

Entering Voice Commands

You can switch to Voice Command by saying "voice command", or to Dictation by saying "dictation".

Go to the Tools menu and make sure the Speech option is on.

Click the Voice Command button on the Language bar.

Spoken commands appear here

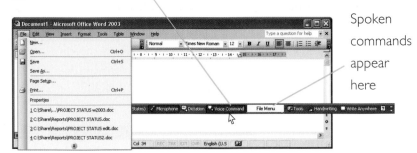

To close a dialog say "OK", to select a toolbar button, say its name and to launch the Task Pane, say "task pane".

Issue the appropriate command. For example, to launch the File menu say "file" or "file menu". To select a menu entry say the name. To open the Font dialog say "font", then to select a typeface, say its name.

Correcting errors

You can also edit incorrectly interpreted text in the normal way.

Right-click on the error. You will see a menu of possible corrections.

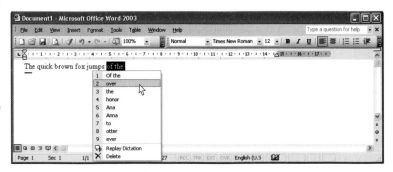

Another way to make a correction is to select the text then, in Dictation mode, make another attempt to say the correct version.

Alternatively, select the erroneous text and, in dictation mode, say "spelling mode", then spell out the correct version of the text.

Tabulation

Text which is laid out with correct and accurate horizontal alignment greatly helps to give a document a professional look.

Effective use of white space, including tabulation, is one of the most important considerations when formatting documents. This chapter deals with a range of tabulation features and examples.

Covers

Default Tabulation | 80

Creating your own Tabulation | 80

The Tabs dialog box | 83

Using Tabs to create Tables | 84

Chapter Seven

Default Tabulation

The default tab stops are set every half-inch. When you press the Tab key, Word automatically moves across the page, stopping when it reaches the next tab stop position.

To see how this works:

Do not feel tempted to space out text by pressing the Spacebar lots of times. This will not produce consistent results, and makes spacing hard to control later on – use tabulation instead.

1 Make sure that the ¶ button is active.

2 Enter items of text separated by a single tab character.

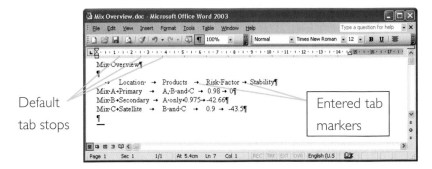

Default tab stops

Entered tab markers

Creating your own Tabulation

1 Select the text.

2 Click in the lower half of the ruler (or the gray bar beneath it) to create a new tab (shaped like an "L") and drag to adjust its position.

To make the ruler display the distances between tab stops when dragging a new tab, hold down the Alt key.

New left tab stop

3 Repeat this process to create more tab stops.

Any new tab stops you create will automatically override the default tabs.

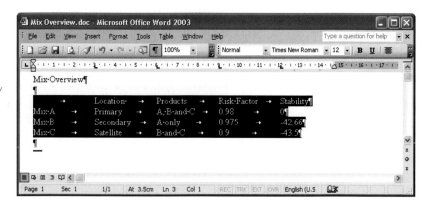

Deleting Tabs

You can delete your tab stops simply by dragging them downwards out of the ruler.

Different types of Tab

You can move your own tab stops at any time by dragging them within the ruler – but be sure to select the main text first.

So far you've created left-aligned tabs, which cause text to align along its left edge under the tab stop.

1 Click the Tab alignment button once to change to center tabs.

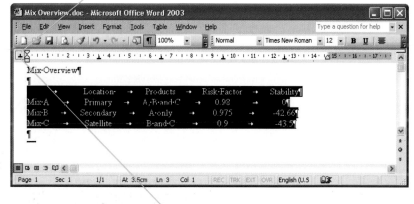

As you click on the Tab Alignment button, it cycles between Left, Center, Right, Decimal alignment, Bar tab, First line indent and, finally, Hanging indent.

2 You can now create centered tabs by clicking in the ruler.

Here is an example of right-aligned tabs:

Tabulation is a paragraph-level attribute. Each paragraph can have its own tab stops if necessary. Make sure that you select all the paragraphs you want to format before setting or modifying tabs.

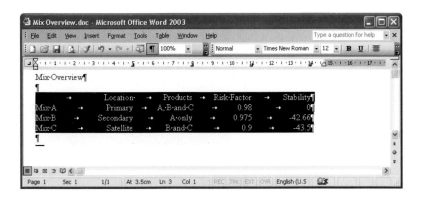

Decimal tabs are used to line up numbers along the decimal point:

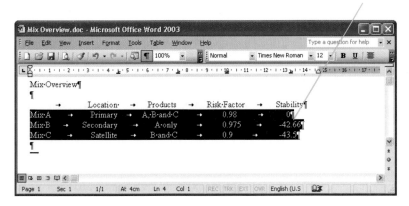

Usually a mixture of different tabs is required:

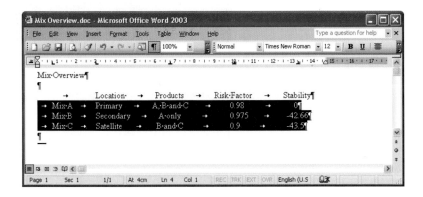

The Tabs dialog box

More options can be found in the Tabs dialog box.

1 Choose Tabs from the Format menu.

2 Set the position and alignment of the tab. You can also fill the tab space with lines or dots using the Leader setting.

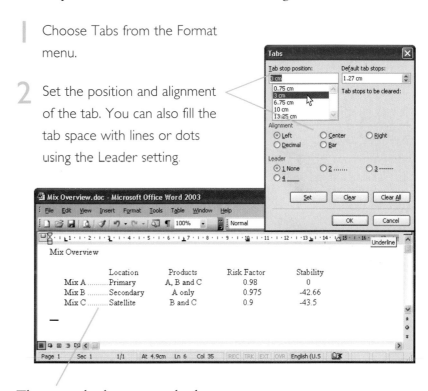

The example above uses a leader consisting of a row of dots.

You can also access the Tabs dialog via the Paragraph dialog.

Bar Tabs

Setting a bar tab causes a vertical line to appear in the text in position.

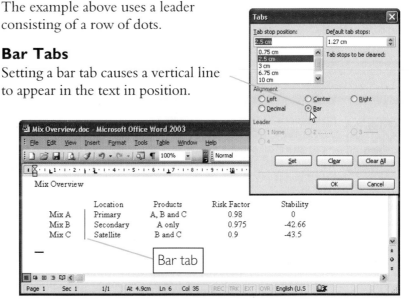

Using Tabs to create Tables

The examples used on the preceding pages have demonstrated the properties of tabs by using them to create a simple table. However, although this table presents a small amount of information clearly, it contains none of the additional effects that are often used to enhance the presentation of tables: borders, shaded cells, etc.

Word does allow you to create tables with these effects, using a very simple click-and-drag method (see Chapter 11 "Tables and charts"), but if you have already entered your table data as we have in this chapter, you won't want to type it in again. Fortunately, you can convert such data into true tables very easily.

1 Highlight the data you want to convert.

2 Go to the Table menu, open the Convert submenu and choose Text to Table.

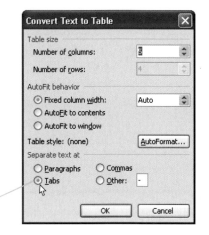

3 If you have separated your columns using tabs, make sure this option is selected.

4 Click OK. The table is created automatically.

HOT TIP

If the width of a column needs adjusting, rest your cursor over the table column icon to its right, then click and drag it to where you want it.

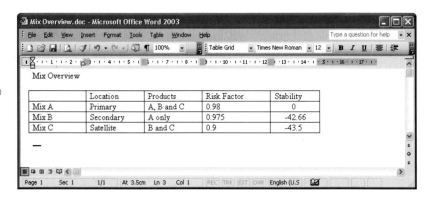

	Location	Products	Risk Factor	Stability
Mix A	Primary	A, B and C	0.98	0
Mix B	Secondary	A only	0.975	-42.66
Mix C	Satellite	B and C	0.9	-43.5

Automatic features

Word has many automatic features which will operate on selected text or a complete document. This chapter looks at many of these, including search and replace tools and facilities for correction of spelling and grammar.

Covers

Find and Replace | 86

Special characters | 91

Spelling and Grammar checking | 92

AutoCorrect | 94

AutoText | 95

The Spike | 96

AutoComplete | 97

Hyphenation | 98

Chapter Eight

Find and Replace

Finding text

Word can be instructed to search through your document for particular words, groups of characters, or formatting attributes.

> Choose Find from the Edit menu, or type Ctrl+F.

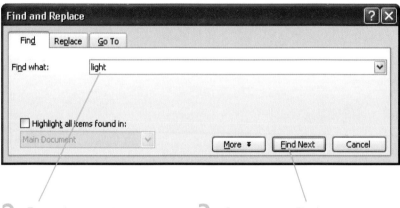

2 Enter the search text.   3 Click on the Find Next button.

Word keeps this dialog box open in case you want to search on to the next occurrence of your text.

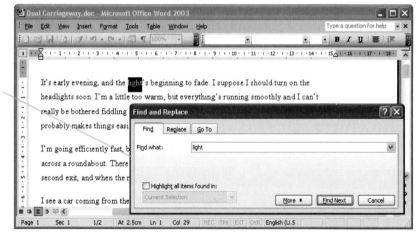

Word will highlight the next instance of the search text within your document. Word will also let you know if the end of the document was reached without it finding any occurrences.

Even if you close the dialog, you can still continue your search by using the two blue buttons in the vertical scrollbar.

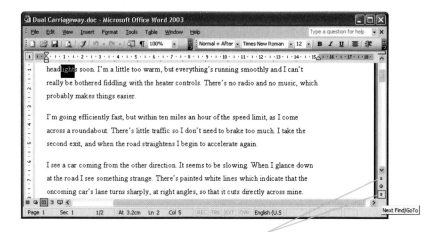

Previous and
Next Find buttons

More or Less

Using the checkboxes in the lower left area of the dialog, you can set Word to look for text in a particular case, for whole words (rather than groups of letters), to use wildcard searching, or phonetic matching.

1   If the Find and Replace dialog is not currently being displayed, then choose Find from the Edit menu, or type Ctrl+F.

2   Click the More button to display more options, or the Less button to see the abbreviated version of this dialog box.

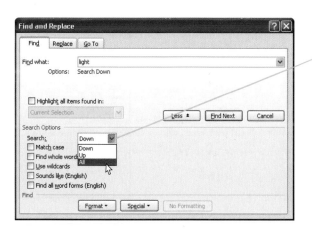

Set the search direction from the insertion point: either downwards, upwards or throughout the entire document.

Searches based on attributes

Your search can be based on attributes as well as specific text. You can even search for particular text and attributes simultaneously.

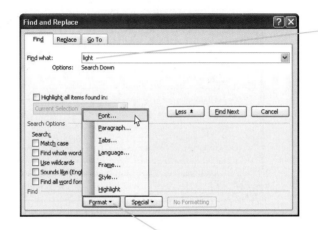

Enter text here, or leave blank if you want to search for any text with specific attributes.

In the Find and Replace dialog box, open the Format drop-down menu and choose the relevant option(s).

This example shows a search for "Times New Roman Italic 12 point" text.

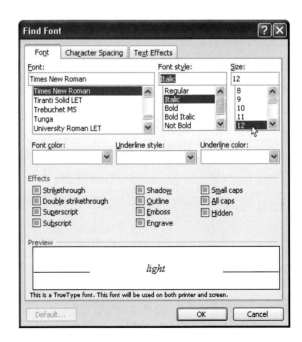

2 Click OK to return to the Find dialog, then click on the Find button to start the search.

Word will now look through your document to find any text which matches *both* what you typed for Find what *and* the attributes you specified:

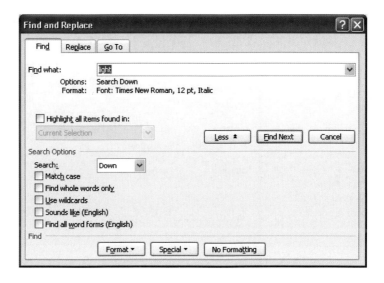

Cancelling attribute searches

If you have previously specified attributes for your search, then you can clear these quickly by clicking on the No Formatting button.

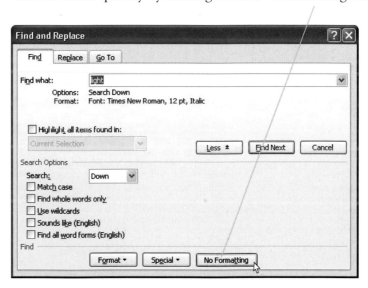

Replacing text

Once you have found an instance of the text you are searching for, you can choose to replace it with some different text.

1 Click on the Replace tab.

2 Enter the Replace with text.

Before clicking on the Format button, be sure to click in either the Find what or Replace with parts of the dialog. This determines whether you want to specify a Format to search for, or to replace with.

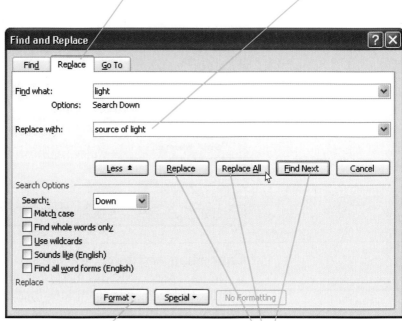

3 If you wish to replace the search text with text that has different format attributes, click here and choose the relevant options.

4 Click Replace to change just this instance of the target text, Replace All to change every instance in the document, or Find Next to skip to the next instance.

To open the Find and Replace dialog with the Replace tab active, you can choose Replace from the Edit menu, or type Ctrl+H. You can then enter the Find what text here before continuing with Step 2. However, if you want to search for text with a particular format, you'll have to use the Find tab.

5 When you're done, click Close.

Special characters

You can use the Special drop-down menu in the Find and Replace tab to easily insert the keyboard codes for special characters.

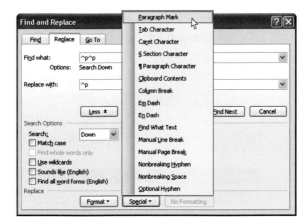

This example shows Word looking for two consecutive paragraph marks, replacing them with a single paragraph mark.

Wildcards

If you want to search, not for a specific piece of text, but for text that follows a certain pattern, select the Use wildcards checkbox before clicking the Special button. You will then find that Special drop-down menu contains some extra entries. For example, to search for words that follow the pattern "g?ve" (where "?" represents any single character), you would do the following:

1 Enter the letter "g" in the Find what box.

2 Click the Special button and select Any Character from the menu.

3 Enter the letters "ve".

This search will highlight all words like "give", "gave", and (if you don't have the Find whole words only checkbox selected) words like "given", too.

Spelling and Grammar checking

Word lets you check your spelling and grammar in two ways: from a special dialog or on-the-fly. The dialog is used as follows:

1 If you don't want to spell check your entire document, then select only the text you require.

The shortcut key for Spelling and Grammar checking is F7.

2 Choose Spelling and Grammar from the Tools menu, or click on the corresponding icon: [icon]

Spelling errors are highlighted in red, grammatical ones in green.

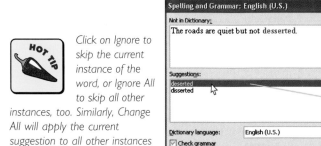

Click on Ignore to skip the current instance of the word, or Ignore All to skip all other instances, too. Similarly, Change All will apply the current suggestion to all other instances as well.

Click one of these (see Hot Tip)

Adds the word to the dictionary

Changes the word to the selected suggestion

Here's an example of Word questioning some grammar:

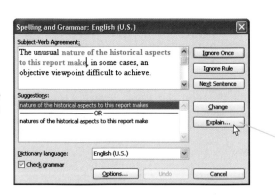

If you disagree with Word's grammar advice, then either click Ignore to skip the current phrase or Ignore Rule to stop Word applying the rule altogether.

If you are unsure about what may be wrong with your grammar, click the Explain button.

3 Clicking the Options button takes you to the Spelling and Grammar options dialog box, where you can customize what Word checks or disable grammar checking.

Checking on-the-fly

While the dialog-box method of checking your spelling and grammar offers you the greatest amount of control over exactly how the checking is done, Word can check your grammar and spelling automatically as you type, highlighting any problems it finds on the page. Consider the following example:

Both the Spelling and the Grammar drop-down menus offer a quick route to the full Spelling and Grammar dialog box: simply select the Spelling entry, or the toolbar icon:

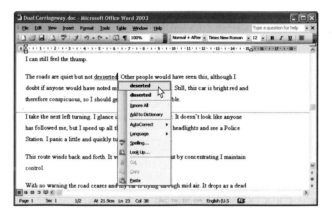

This spelling mistake is underlined in red. To correct, right-click on it then select the correct suggested word from the drop-down menu. If the suggestion is not suitable, attempt to correct it yourself, then see if it is still flagged.

You can display readability statistics after performing a Spelling and Grammar check. Select Options from the Tools menu and choose the Spelling and Grammar tab. Make sure that Show readability statistics is checked, then click OK.

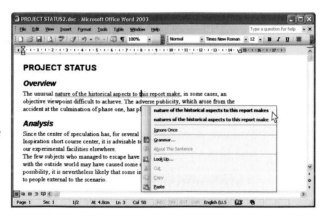

This grammar mistake is underlined in green. Right-click on it, then select the correct suggestion from the menu.

AutoCorrect

Often, the same spelling or typing mistakes are made again and again. You can instruct Word to substitute the correction automatically.

You don't have to enter all the AutoCorrect data yourself: Word contains a large number of corrections, including common mistakes for "necessary", "occasion", and transposition errors such as "knwo" instead of "know". You can browse through these from the AutoCorrect dialog.

1   Choose AutoCorrect Options from the Tools menu, and make sure that this tab is selected.

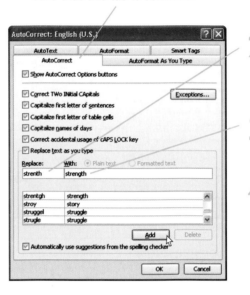

2   Enter the commonly mistyped version of the word here...

3   ...and the correct version here.

4   Click Add, then repeat for any other mapped corrections. When you are done, click OK.

If you type the error now, Word spots it and substitutes the correct word automatically, instead of merely flagging it as a possible spelling mistake:

| Identified strenths | | Identified strengths |

Original text typed   *Corrected by Word*

To summarize the active document, open the Tools menu and choose AutoSummarize. Word carries out the initial analysis. When it's completed, select a summary option (e.g. Create a new document...). Enter a percentage and click OK.

You can now continue through the rest of your life completely unaware that you are consistently failing to spell correctly.

AutoSummarize

In effect, Word provides another way to view a document: you can "summarize" it. When you summarize a document, Word analyzes it and allocates a "score" to each sentence. You then specify what percentage of the higher scoring sentences should be displayed.

AutoText

This is a less automatic version of AutoCorrect, and is useful for setting up your own abbreviations.

If you find that you often need to type the same text, then it would be worth setting up an AutoText entry.

Creating an AutoText entry

1 Type the text and select it.

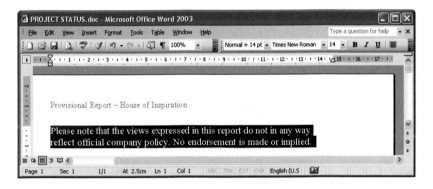

Note that you can also use the AutoText toolbar button:
If it isn't visible, you can display it by checking the AutoText entry in the View>Toolbars menu.

2 Choose AutoCorrect Options from the Tools menu and select the AutoText tab.

3 Edit the entry in this box to the required abbreviation.

4 Click OK.

The selected text is automatically inserted into this area of the AutoText dialog box.

Using AutoText

Simply type the abbreviation:

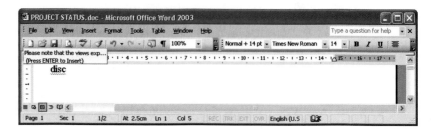

2 Press Enter or F3 to replace the abbreviation with the text.

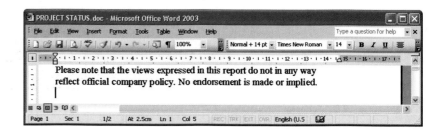

The Spike

The Spike is a temporary piece of AutoText which can be added to with a single key command.

Creating a Spike

You can repeat this more times if necessary. Each time you press Ctrl+F3, any selected text is added to the Spike.

1 Select some text and type Ctrl+F3. The text disappears. It has been impaled on the Spike.

2 Repeat the process with a second piece of text.

3 Finally, place the insertion point at the destination for the text and press Control+Shift+F3. The text is pulled off the Spike and placed back into the document.

AutoComplete

AutoComplete is somewhat akin to AutoText, in that it offers suggestions for the completion of words or phrases that you only need to begin typing. However, while AutoText uses a list of commonly used phrases which have first to be recorded, AutoComplete offers to fill in other types of text which can be worked out from the context. For example, AutoComplete can enter:

- the current date

- your name

- your company's name

- any day of the week

- any month

Begin to type in one of the words or phrases listed above.

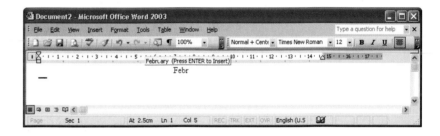

AutoComplete offers to fill in the complete text.

To accept the AutoComplete suggestion press Enter or F3.

If AutoComplete doesn't appear to be functioning, choose AutoCorrect Options from the Tools menu. Select the AutoText tab, and make sure that Show AutoComplete suggestions is checked.

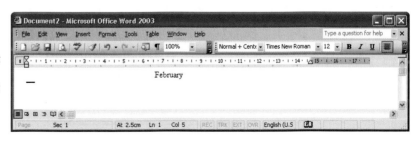

Hyphenation

1 You can change the hyphenation options for your document by opening the Tools menu, choosing Language and then Hyphenation.

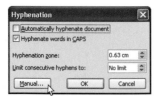

2 If you click on the Manual button you can review hyphenation manually throughout your document.

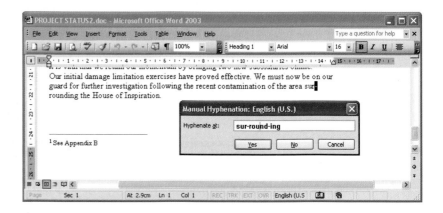

To take even greater control of hyphenation in your text, you may want to use the following keyboard shortcuts: Ctrl+Hyphen will insert an optional hyphen in a word as you type; Ctrl+Shift+Hyphen will insert a non-breaking hyphen into your text (this is a hyphen where Word is not allowed to break the text over successive lines).

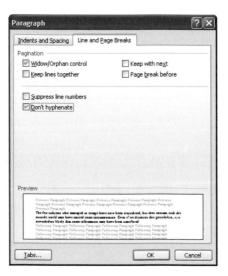

You can also override hyphenation for individual paragraphs by selecting the Don't hyphenate checkbox in the Line and Page Breaks tab of the Paragraph dialog box (choose Paragraph from the Format menu).

Templates and Wizards

Templates act as blueprints for standard types of document which you might need to use again and again. Examples may be standard memos, reports, letters or faxes. A Wizard is a "live" document which guides you through its own design.

This chapter shows you how to use templates and Wizards, customize a template for your own purposes, or create a new template.

Covers

Using templates | 100

Template defaults | 101

Form templates | 102

Setting up a new template | 105

Changing Styles in a template | 106

The Templates and Add-ins dialog | 106

Wizards | 107

Chapter Nine

Using templates

A template contains a range of settings to be used as a starting point for a new document.

The normal and general templates

If you select the New icon 🔲 *instead of the File menu, Word uses the Normal template to create a new blank document.*

1 Choose New from the File menu.

Word makes the Task Pane visible, displaying its New Document controls.

2 Choose On my computer from the Templates section in the Task Pane.

Word lists the templates available. Often you'll use the simple Blank Document template (listed in the General tab).

3 Click on the other tabs to see more available templates.

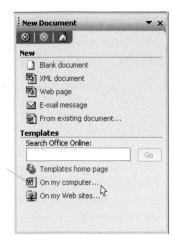

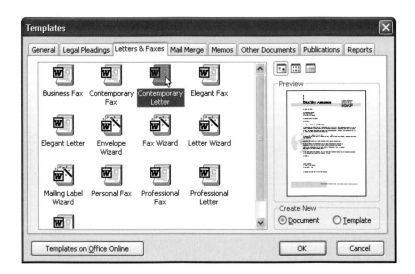

4 Select the template you want to use and click OK.

Template defaults

Defaults are settings which are used initially when you create a new document or add new text. To change the defaults for a template, do the following with a template open:

1 Open the Font dialog box from the Format menu.

2 Choose your required settings and then click on the Default button.

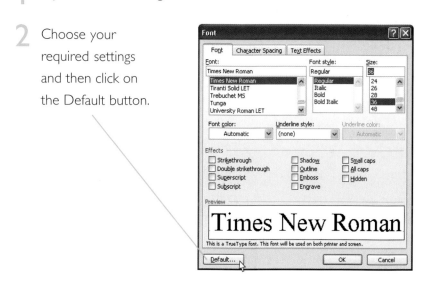

A dialog box will ask you whether you're certain that you want to change the template itself.

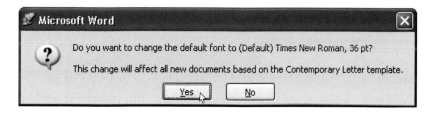

3 If you click Yes, the font information will be saved into the currently used template document.

Form templates

By designing a Form template, you can create a document which is very easy to use, even for people who have minimal experience of Word.

You simply create a document in the normal way, apart from adding some special "form fields". These can be text containers, checkboxes or drop-down selection fields.

Creating Text Form Fields

1 Make sure the Forms palette is active (if necessary go to the View menu and choose Toolbars>Forms).

2 Place your insertion point where you'd like the field, then click on the Text Form Field button in the Forms palette.

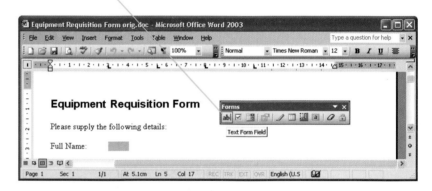

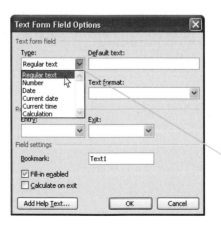

3 With the Text Form field still selected, click on the Form Field Options button:

From here you can select options such as the content type.

Creating Drop-down Form Fields

Drop-down lists allow users to select from a restricted list of options. This way they can fill out values within a form without typing anything.

1 Position your insertion point where you'd like the field to be.

2 Click on the Drop-Down Form Field icon in the Forms palette.

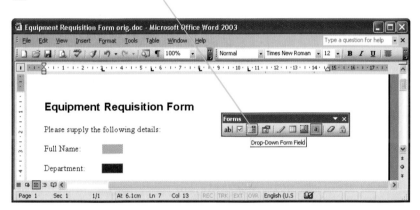

3 With the field still selected, click on the Form Field Options button:

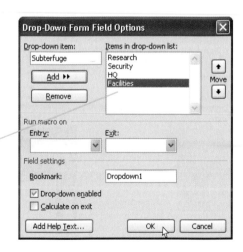

From here you can build the list of values for the drop-down list. Simply enter an item and click the Add button. You can also use the Move buttons to reorder the items or remove items altogether.

4 When the list is complete, click OK.

Creating Check Box Form Fields

These act as simple on/off switches for your user. A single-click will toggle a checkmark on and off within the box.

1 Position your insertion point where you'd like the field.

2 Click the Check Box Form Field icon in the Forms palette.

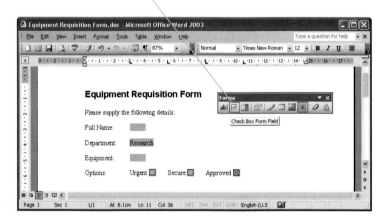

Protecting the Form

1 Click on the Protect Form icon to stop users from editing your document. From now onwards the only items which can be edited are the Form Fields themselves.

Close down the Forms Toolbar when you've completed your form. This will hopefully discourage users from attempting to edit the document.

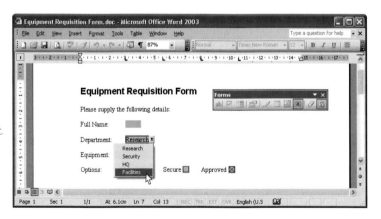

Setting up a new template

Any document can be saved as a template, but in this example we'll use the form we've created. With the document open, do the following:

You can also switch protection on and off using the Forms Toolbar. However, in the Task pane there are additional controls for locking just parts of the document, and specifying precisely who is allowed to make changes.

1 If the document is not already protected, select Protect Document from the Tools menu. The Task pane will open (if not already open) and switch to the Protect Document controls.

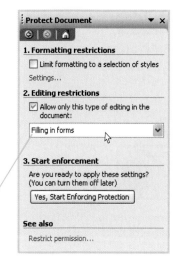

2 Under the Editing restrictions settings, switch on the Allow only... checkbox and choose Filling in forms from the menu.

You only need to do this if the template is to be used as a form.

If you're making a template using a normal document, rather than a form, you need only follow Steps 3 and 4.

3 Choose Save As from the File menu:

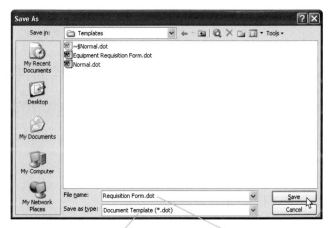

Documents saved as templates will be automatically created with a .DOT extension within Word's Templates folder. This makes them available later on when you choose to create a new document from a template.

4 Choose Document Template as the file type.

5 Enter a suitable name for the file and click on Save.

Changing Styles in a template

If the Styles and Formatting section of the Task pane is not visible, you can activate it by choosing Styles and Formatting from the Format menu.

When you open a document, Word uses the styles built into the template selected. As shown earlier, you can alter these styles for individual documents using the Style dialog:

1 In the Styles and Formatting section of the Task pane, choose a style then select Modify from its drop-down menu. This dialog appears.

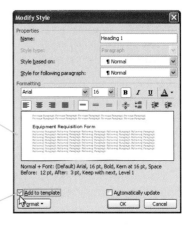

If you record a style change to the Blank Document or Normal template, this will affect most new documents.

2 To copy a style change back into the template itself, make sure the Add to template box is checked.

The Templates and Add-ins dialog

Word keeps track of the template used to create a document. It is possible to change this even after you've started work.

1 If necessary, unprotect your document (Tools menu).

2 Choose Templates and Add-Ins from the Tools menu.

You can use the Add button to make available styles stored in other templates. Any templates listed in the Global box are always available.

3 Use the Attach button to attach a new template. If you select Automatically Update Document Styles then the styles from the new template will be reapplied to the document text.

4 Click OK when you're done.

Wizards

Another useful example is the Fax Wizard. Word is actually capable of sending out faxes directly, provided you have a fax-capable modem properly installed in your system. If you are not set up for this, however, you can still get the Wizard to create a document which you would firstly print, then send manually using a Fax machine.

A Wizard is a kind of "intelligent" template: it helps you design and build a document by asking you a series of questions. You answer these, either by selecting from a choice of radio buttons, or by entering text in a box.

An example

1 If you can't see the New Document controls in the Task Pane, choose New from the File menu.

2 Under Templates choose On my computer.

3 Select the Other Documents tab in the Templates dialog box. Click on the Calendar Wizard icon, then click OK.

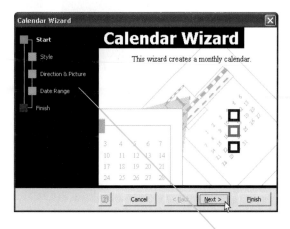

4 Start working through the Wizard by clicking the Next button.

5 Each page of the Wizard will ask you questions. As you work through, the flowchart on the left will show your progress.

6 At any point you can go back to a previous page simply by clicking the Back button. This way you can fill out the settings in any order you choose.

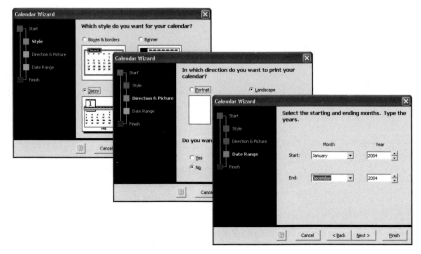

Many more templates are available online via the Web. You can browse through those on Microsoft Office Online by clicking on the Templates home page link in the Task bar.

7 The final step is to click Finish.

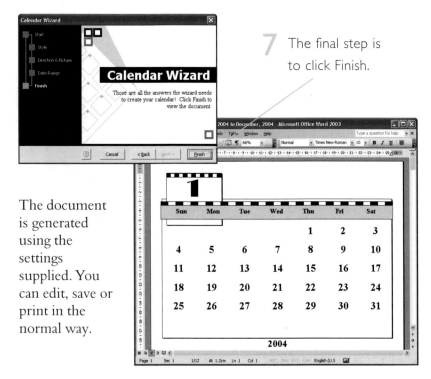

The document is generated using the settings supplied. You can edit, save or print in the normal way.

Graphical features

Although not a full-blown graphics package, Word contains a comprehensive collection of clip art as well as a respectable range of graphical editing features. This chapter takes you through the processes involved with incorporating pictures and illustrations into your document.

Covers

Inserting pictures from disk | 110

Inserting Clip Art | 111

Manipulating graphics | 112

The Picture toolbar | 113

Cropping a picture | 113

Editing an imported picture | 114

Wrapping text around graphics | 115

The Format Picture dialog | 116

The Drawing toolbar | 116

Creating shapes | 117

Lines and fills | 117

AutoShapes | 118

Changing object order | 119

Grouping and ungrouping | 120

WordArt | 121

Chapter Ten

Inserting pictures from disk

Word can import many types of graphic file format. WMF, CGM, WPG, DRW, EPS and PCT files normally contain draw-type objects which can be scaled up or down with no loss in quality, because they are stored as vectors (mathematical objects). On the other hand BMP, PCX, TIF, JPG and GIF files are bitmapped: the image is stored as a structure of tiny dots or blocks. Be careful not to enlarge these pictures too much, or the dots will become very noticeable, causing a marked deterioration in quality.

Word has its own supply of clip art illustrations (see the next page), but you can also import from a wide range of graphic formats.

1   Click the insertion point at the destination for the graphic.

2   Go to the Insert menu, choose Picture and From File.

3   Locate the file you require and click Insert.

By default, Word will embed a copy of the graphic in your file. This will allow you to make changes to the graphic within Word, but tends to make your files larger. If you choose the Link to File option (by clicking on the downward-pointing arrow at the right hand side of the Insert button), then Word doesn't store its own local copy. This keeps your Word files smaller, but make sure that you keep the original graphic file where Word can find it.

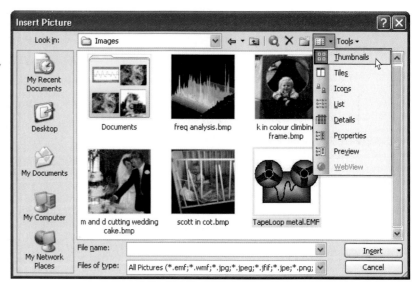

4   Once inserted, pictures (and clip art) can be moved or resized in the normal way.

Inserting Clip Art

Using the Insert Clip Art Task Pane

You can use Click and Type to insert pictures in blank page areas.

Clips have associated keywords. You can use these to locate clips.

You can add new clips to collections (or add new keywords to existing clips) in the Clip Organizer. Click here to launch it.

For access to more clips, select Clip art on Office Online and follow the instructions.

1 First, position the insertion point at the location within the active document where you want to insert the picture.

2 Pull down the Insert menu and choose Picture, Clip Art. The Task Pane will show the Clip Art controls.

3 Enter one or more keywords and, optionally, make choices for the other two pop-up menus to limit the results. When you are ready click Search. The results will display in the main part of the Task pane.

4 Click on an image to insert it. Alternatively you may wish to click on the image's pop-up menu first, and choose Preview/ Properties before deciding on whether to bring it into your document.

Manipulating graphics

When you click on a graphic you'll see 8 blocks around it: 1 at each corner and 1 at the middle of each side. These are the graphic's control handles, which can be used to change its dimensions.

If you have a scanner or a digital camera connected to your system, you can scan directly into Word. Choose Insert>Picture then From Scanner or Camera.

Click on the graphic to make its handles appear.

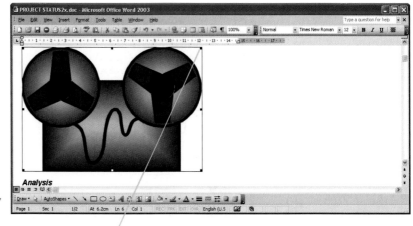

Word creates a "Drawing Canvas" on which graphic elements sit. If graphic elements are created on the same canvas, then it is much easier to move them together. You can tell when the canvas is present by its thick shaded border and corner "crop handles" (see below). You can move the whole canvas by dragging with the mouse on the border. Dragging on the corner "crop handles" lets you resize the canvas area.

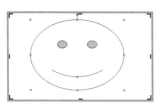

Drag on a handle to resize the picture.

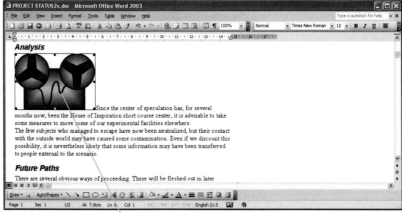

To move, drag anywhere within the object.

Note that the graphic is treated like a text item, so when you drag it to a new position, the surrounding text moves to make room.

The Picture toolbar

The Picture toolbar appears when you insert a picture into a
document and provides an easy way of making a wide range of
changes to your pictures. Use it for the following functions:

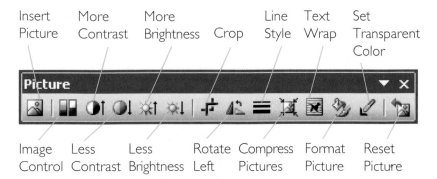

Insert Picture • More Contrast • More Brightness • Crop • Line Style • Text Wrap • Set Transparent Color

Image Control • Less Contrast • Less Brightness • Rotate Left • Compress Pictures • Format Picture • Reset Picture

Cropping a picture

If you want to display only part of an image in your Word
document, you should crop it. This cuts away a part of the picture.

1 Select the image.

2 Click on the Crop icon.

Cropping is non-destructive. This means that you can restore the rest of the picture by dragging the edges back with the Crop tool, or by clicking on the Reset Picture icon (in the Picture Toolbar).

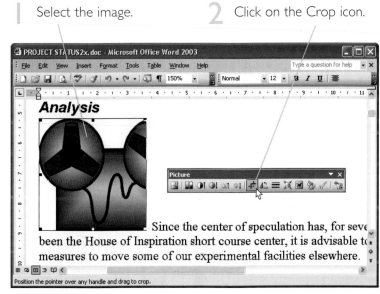

3 Rest your cursor over any of the picture's control handles, then drag the edges to where you want them.

Editing an imported picture

Most normal clip art that you import will be in vector format, which means it can be broken down into simple individual elements which can be edited separately. To edit a vector clip art image, do the following:

Most Office Clip Art files have a .WMF or .EMF extension. These stand for Windows MetaFile and Enhanced MetaFile respectively.

1 Right-click on the image and choose Edit Picture.

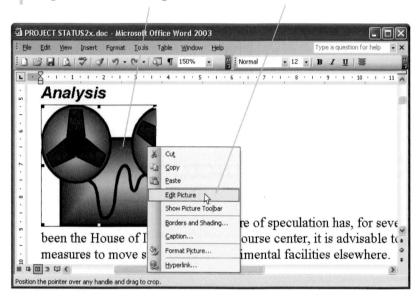

2 Right-click on the image and choose Edit Picture.

If you extend the picture beyond its normal bounding rectangle, click on the Fit icon in the Drawing Canvas Toolbar to reset the picture boundary. If you cannot see the Drawing Canvas Toolbar, right-click on the patterned gray border of the Drawing Canvas, and choose Show Drawing Canvas Toolbar from the pop-up menu which appears.

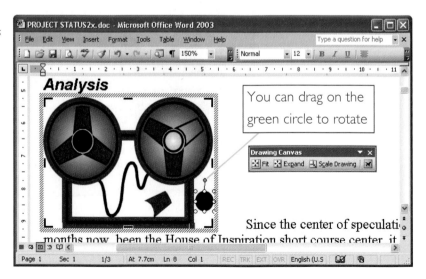

Wrapping text around graphics

When a graphic is inserted into a Word document, it is placed into the text by default as a simple object, on a new line. However, you can very easily change this, so that text wraps around the image in any of a number of ways.

1   Select the picture.

2   Click on the Text Wrap icon in the Picture toolbar, and select how you want the text to wrap around the image.

If the Picture Toolbar is not visible, select Toolbars from the View menu (or right-click on any visible Toolbar), and choose Picture.

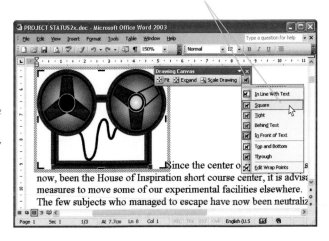

The text now wraps around the image. This is '"Square" wrap: the text wraps around a rectangular area that borders the graphic.

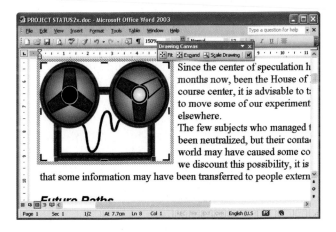

The Format Picture dialog

From here you can numerically change all the properties of a graphic, including its size, position, text-wrap properties and crop parameters.

1 Select the picture.

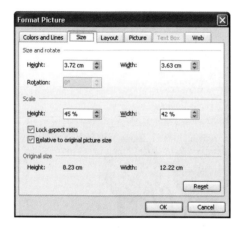

2 Choose the Format Picture icon from the Picture toolbar:

3 Select the appropriate tab.

4 Make your changes, then click OK to apply them.

The Drawing toolbar

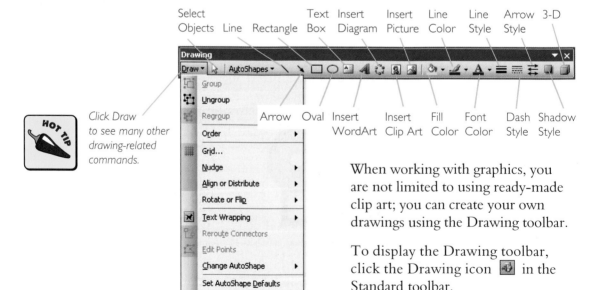

Click Draw to see many other drawing-related commands.

When working with graphics, you are not limited to using ready-made clip art; you can create your own drawings using the Drawing toolbar.

To display the Drawing toolbar, click the Drawing icon in the Standard toolbar.

Creating shapes

1 Select the appropriate shape tool.

2 Click and drag within the document to create the shape.

When creating shapes by dragging with the mouse: for lines, drag from one end-point to the other; for boxes and ovals drag diagonally from one corner to the other.

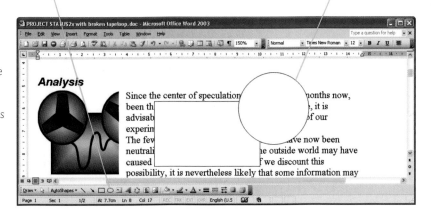

3 Click on a shape with the pointer to select it. Then drag it to another location or resize it by dragging directly on a handle.

Lines and fills

Click on a shape then use the Fill and Line drop-down menus to select color, shading and line patterns.

1 Click the arrow just right of the icon to show the menu.

2 Click here to access more line options.

These properties can also be changed using the Format AutoShape dialog box: right-click on a shape, then select Format AutoShape from the drop-down menu.

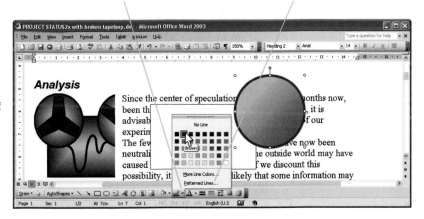

AutoShapes

AutoShapes let you insert common shapes which otherwise might take some time to draw. To insert an AutoShape, do the following:

If you plan to use several AutoShapes in one session, you can simply drag one of the submenu palettes away from the main menu, to create a floating palette. It will then stay on-screen when the AutoShapes menu disappears.

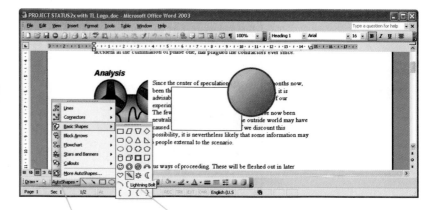

1 Click on the AutoShapes button.

2 Select an AutoShapes category, then click on a specific shape.

3 Click in the area of your document where you want the AutoShape to appear.

Many object properties can be amended by accessing the drop-down menus in the Drawing toolbar. However, by right-clicking on a shape you can summon a dialog box that allows you to change many of these properties straight away. Right-click on the object whose format you want to change, choose Format AutoShape from the drop-down menu, then select the appropriate tab.

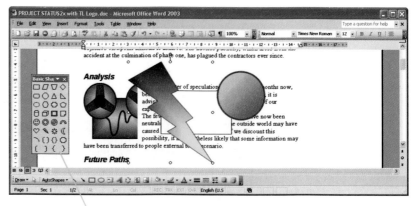

Free-floating Shapes palette

Changing object order

When you place a new image or shape in a document, it appears in front of all the other objects. To change the relative order of objects subsequently, select the object(s) to move, then:

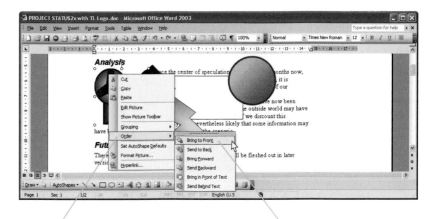

1 Right-click on a shape and choose Order from the menu.

2 Choose to send the object in front of or behind all other objects, or to move it just one step.

Sending objects behind the Text Layer

By default, all graphic objects appear in front of the text in your document. However, you can send objects behind the text by selecting Send Behind Text from the menu shown above.

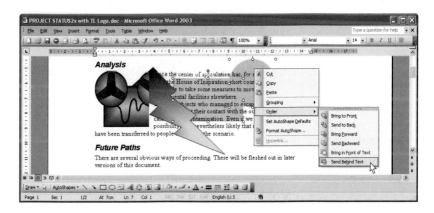

Grouping and ungrouping

Once you have placed several objects in your Word document, you may no longer need to treat them separately, but you might benefit from treating them as a single object which can be moved and modified easily. To do this, you can group the objects, as follows:

There are two basic ways of selecting a series of objects: click successively on each object while holding down the Shift button, or click in a vacant part of the document area and drag a selection box around all of the objects.

1 Select all of the objects that you want to be grouped together.

2 Choose Group in the Draw menu in the Drawing toolbar.

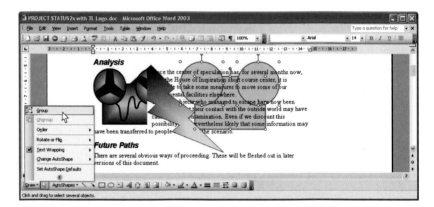

Any changes to the group are applied to all the grouped objects:

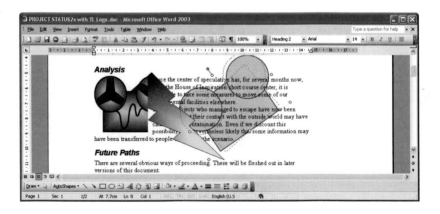

WordArt

WordArt is a tool you can use to apply a wide range of special graphical effects to text that you use in your Word documents. The objects created by WordArt are treated, not as plain text, but as drawing objects, so they can be manipulated further with the tools from the Drawing toolbar. To use WordArt, do the following:

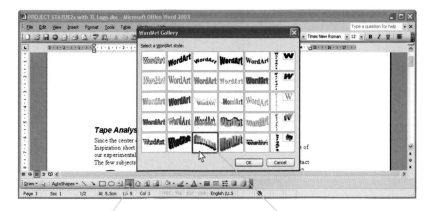

1 Click on the WordArt button in the Drawing toolbar.

2 Select a style (you can change it later) then OK.

3 Enter your text here, then click OK.

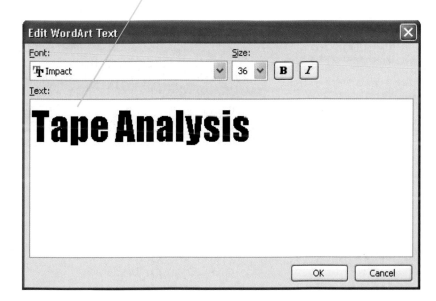

The WordArt object is placed, and can now be edited:

Remember that by dragging on this small green circle you can freely rotate your object. This applies to AutoShapes as well as WordArt objects.

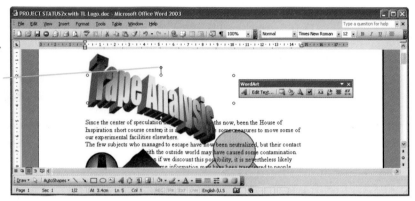

4 Click on the text and drag it to the desired position.

5 Drag on the text's control handles to resize it.

6 Drag the yellow handles to alter the effect's attributes.

The floating WordArt toolbar appears whenever you select a WordArt object. You can use it for the following functions:

Edit text again   Alter color, size, position, text wrap   Edit text wrapping   Toggle between horizontal and vertical

Add a new item   Select a new style   Change shape   Make letters same height   Realign   Change character spacing

When you select the Change shape icon, you are presented with a palette containing 40 different text shapes. This offers a wider range of shapes than the Gallery:

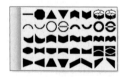

Tables and charts

Tables allow you to organize and manage text in rows and columns. Charts provide a valuable way of presenting numeric table information in pictorial form, making statistical information much easier to understand.

Covers

Inserting a table | 124

Drawing a table | 125

Entering text | 127

Formatting | 128

Inserting a row/column | 128

Cutting and pasting/merging cells | 129

Controlling height and width | 130

Nested tables | 130

Formulae | 131

Borders and shading | 132

Table AutoFormat | 134

The Tables and Borders toolbar | 135

Graphics within tables | 136

Text wrap around tables | 136

Creating a chart from a table | 137

Formatting a chart | 138

Importing data into a chart | 140

Chapter Eleven

Inserting a table

If you want to insert a simple table you can use the Table icon in the Standard toolbar.

Another way to create a table is to select Insert Table from the Table menu. This will summon a dialog box, where you can specify the table's dimensions along with other useful attributes.

1   Place the insertion point on a blank line in the document.

2   Click on the Table icon in the Standard toolbar and, in the drop-down table box, drag downwards and to the right.

You can resize a column by moving your mouse pointer to the border between the columns: it will turn into a black double-headed arrow: You can resize rows in the same way.

The further you drag, the larger the table. In this case a table of 4 rows and 3 columns is being created. The table is inserted into your document.

Hold down the Alt key while dragging a column or row in order to see a continuous readout of current sizes in the ruler.

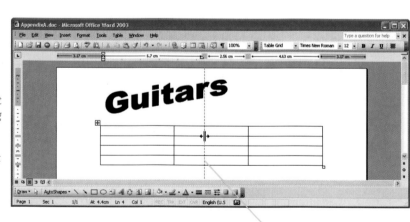

This column is being resized.

Drawing a table

There is an alternative way to begin drawing a table and specify the width of its columns visually: in normal text-entry mode, enter a line using plus and minus symbols, like this:

---+------+------+

When you press Return, Word will automatically convert this into the first line of a table, the plus signs becoming column boundaries. If this doesn't work, select Tools>AutoCorrect, choose the AutoFormat As You Type tab, and check the Tables box.

Word offers an alternative method to create tables. The Draw Table tool lets you draw a table directly into your document without using dialogs or drop-down boxes.

1 Select Table>Draw Table to see the Tables and Borders Toolbar.

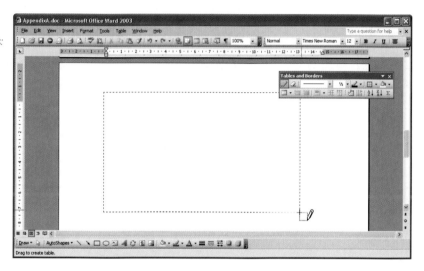

2 Your pointer will turn into a pencil shape. Drag an initial shape for the table within your document.

If you want to draw table edges and your pointer is not already in the shape of a pencil, click on this icon in the Tables and Borders toolbar.

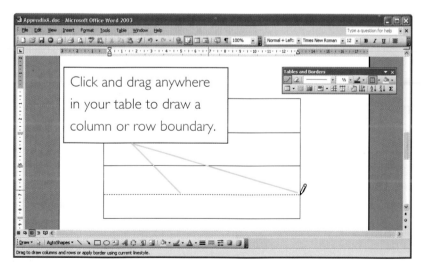

Drawing diagonal table lines

The Draw Table tool will also let you draw diagonally within a table.

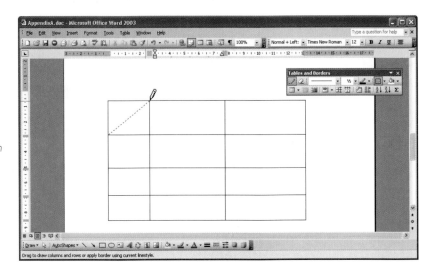

Erasing table lines

Click on the Eraser tool in the Tables and Borders palette. Your cursor turns into an eraser shape.

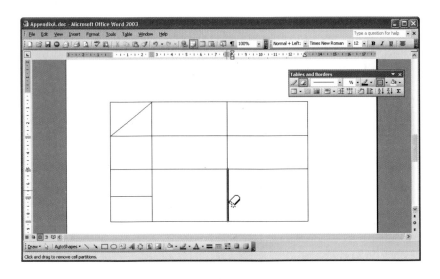

2 Click directly on a line within the table to make it disappear.

Creating irregular tables

The table drawing tools make it easy to create irregularly structured tables.

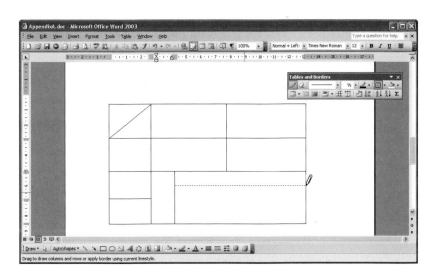

Entering text

If you actually need to enter a Tab character within a table's cell, press Ctrl+Tab. Note that just pressing tab will instead take you to the next cell.

To add text to your table click in each cell in turn then type. All normal formatting commands still apply. A quick way to get to the next cell is to press Tab. Shift+Tab takes you back to the previous cell.

You can have more than one line within each cell. The Table row will expand to accommodate any extra text.

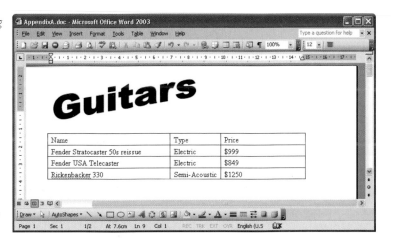

Formatting

You can format the contents of a whole row or column – or several rows or columns – at once. To select a row, drag across it, or click in the space just to its left.

The same applies to columns. To select, click slightly above the top cell to select an entire column for formatting.

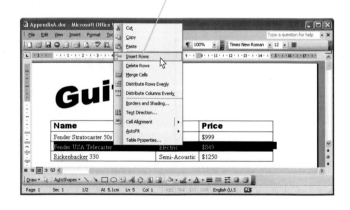

Make any formatting changes to selected cells.

Row height changes automatically to accommodate the text.

Inserting a row/column

To insert a row into an existing table, do the following:

To add a column, first select the column to the right of where you want to insert.

1 Select the line below where you want the new row.

2 Click the right mouse button on the selected row, and choose Insert Rows from the drop-down menu.

To insert multiple columns or rows, select the amount of columns/rows you want inserted before right-clicking.

Cutting and pasting

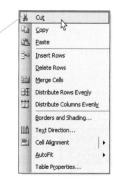

1 Select the row/column or cells.

2 Right-click on the selected cells and choose Cut from the drop-down menu.

3 Select the destination row/column or cells.

4 Right click and choose Paste or Paste Rows from the drop-down menu.

The text is pasted back into the table, immediately above the selected row, or to the left of the selected column.

Merging cells

Any number of adjacent cells can be merged to create a single cell. Select the cells and then choose Table>Merge Cells.

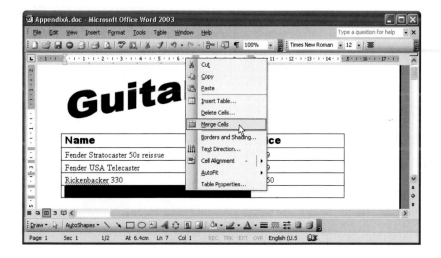

Controlling height and width

1 Select the cell(s) to change, or the entire table.

2 Choose Table Properties from the Table menu, or by right-clicking.

To select an entire table, choose Select, then Table from the Table menu, or type Alt+Numeric keypad "5" with Num Lock turned off.

3 Click on the Row tab, then the Column tab to see all the options available.

4 The Table Tab will let you set properties such as overall size, alignment and text wrap behavior.

Nested tables

It is also possible to insert a table within another table. You can draw the inner table in the normal way with the Draw Table tool:

Another way to create a nested table is to right-click on the destination cell and choose Insert Table. You can also cut, copy and paste entire tables.

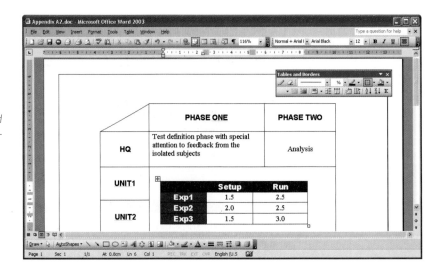

Formulae

If you want one cell of a table to display a number derived from a calculation (based on the numeric contents of other cells), Word can insert a code to perform this task automatically. Here, we want to total the price of the three guitars in the table.

For the Sum function to work properly, all rows above the current cell must have the same number of columns. If you merged the cells for the last example, you will need to split them again (choose Split Cells from the Table menu).

1. Click in the cell which is the destination for the calculation, and choose Formula from the Table menu.

2. Enter the formula or select from the list of Paste functions. Word correctly suggests the =SUM(ABOVE) function, which adds up the contents of the cells above the destination cell.

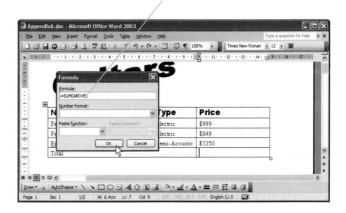

Unlike a spreadsheet (such as Excel), Word does not automatically update the contents of cells containing a formula when the values of cells used in the equation are changed. To update a formula, right-click on the cell and choose Update Field from the drop-down menu.

3. Click OK. The total is displayed in the destination cell.

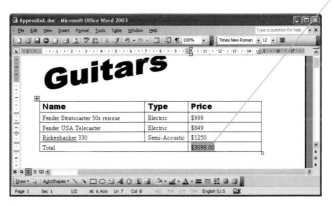

Borders and shading

Word allows you to enhance your tables very easily, using the Borders and Shading dialog. To use it, do the following:

1 Select either the entire table or just a range of cells.

2 Right-click on the selected cells and choose Borders and Shading from the drop-down menu.

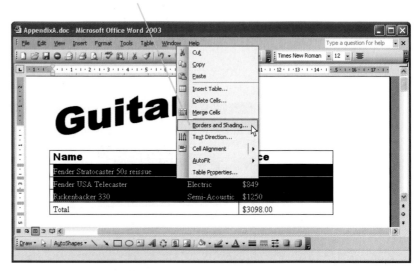

3 If necessary, activate the Borders tab and choose your borders options.

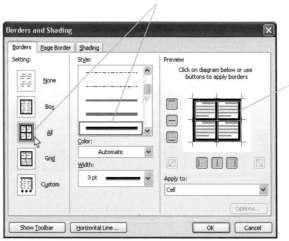

You can click various parts of this diagram to activate perimeter and internal lines.

4 Now click on the Shading tab and set your shading preferences.

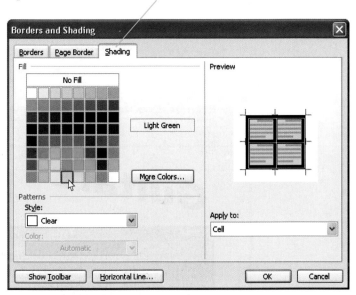

5 Click OK. Your selected cells now have a border and shading applied.

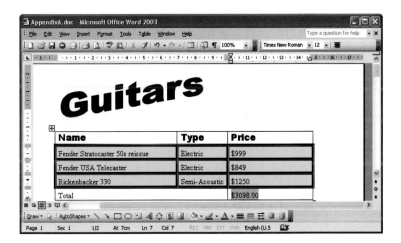

In the example above, the Borders and Shading dialog box has been used to alter the style of all the lines in the selected area, and to give those cells a fill of light green.

Table AutoFormat

As an alternative to defining the format piece by piece (i.e. specifying the font, borders, shading, etc.), Word allows you to apply many different pre-defined formats to existing tables.

1 Select the table.

2 Choose Table AutoFormat from the Table menu, or click on this button.

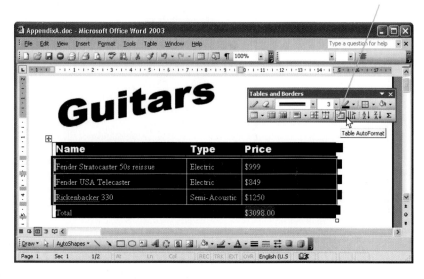

The AutoFormat preview reflects the changes you are about to make.

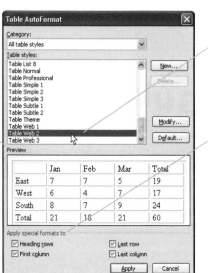

3 Choose a Format style.

4 Select the elements to which AutoFormat should apply.

5 Click Apply to confirm your changes.

The changes just specified are applied automatically to your table.

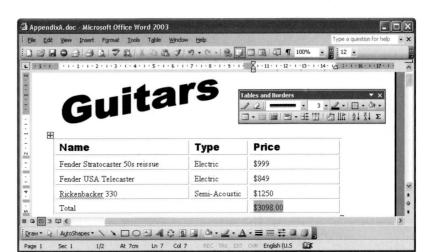

The Tables and Borders toolbar

You can use the Tables and Borders toolbar to make many of the formatting changes discussed earlier in this chapter. If it is not already activated, select View>Toolbars>Tables and Borders, or click on the appropriate icon in the Standard toolbar:

The Tables and Borders toolbar offers the following functions:

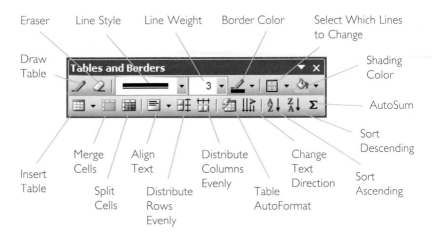

Graphics within tables

You can paste or insert graphics directly into cells, as in this example, then you can right-click on the graphic and choose Format Picture to control properties such as text wrap.

Text and graphics can coexist in the same cell, as illustrated in this example.

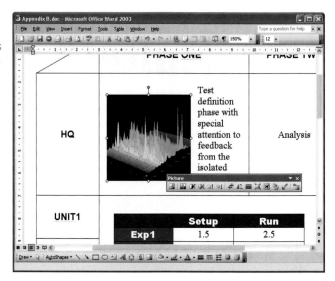

Text wrap around tables

If you right-click on a table and choose Table Properties, you can control how text wraps around the table itself. In the example below, a text wrap setting of Around allows the table to be included within the main text area.

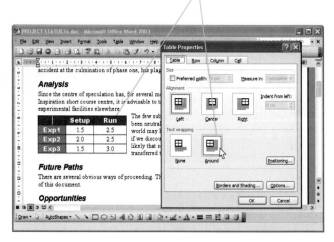

Creating a chart from a table

You can use the Microsoft Graph feature to convert a table you
have created into an attractive chart.

| Select the data in the table.

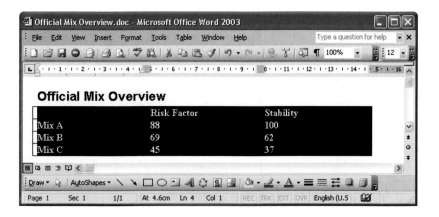

2 Choose Object from the Insert Menu.

3 Choose Microsoft Graph Chart from the Create New tab of the
Object dialog, then click OK.

*You can also
activate the Chart
application by
clicking on the
Chart tool:*
*If this is not visible, right-click on
a toolbar and choose Customize.
The Chart icon is available under
the Insert category. From here
you can drag it onto any toolbar.*

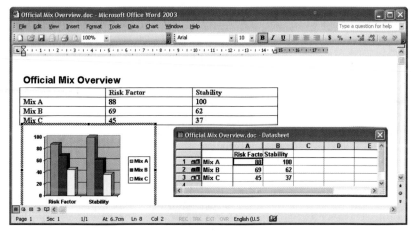

Microsoft Graph automatically generates a suitable graph based on
your data, and places it in your document.

Formatting a chart

Once your chart is in your document, you can very easily edit it to change the format that Microsoft Graph applied by default.

If you can't locate this icon, then you can access the same options from Chart Type in the Chart menu.

1 Double-click on a chart to edit it. A striped border appears and special Microsoft Graph icons appear in the toolbar.

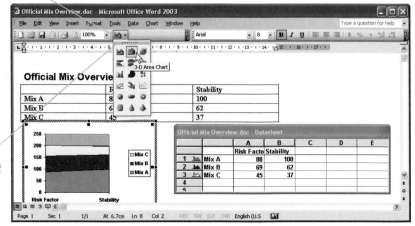

You can make this a free-floating palette by dragging it into the main window.

2 To change the type of chart, click on the arrow to the right of the Chart type icon and select an option from the palette.

3 Click here to close the palette when you've finished with it.

Microsoft uses two main windows, one for the data and one for the chart itself. You can turn the Datasheet on and off using the View menu, or the Datasheet icon on the toolbar:

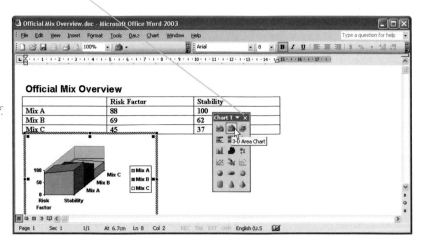

4 To change the properties of a 3-D graph, rest the cursor over the chart area until the Chart Area bubble appears, then right-click.

Clicking here would produce a dialog that offers an alternative way of selecting the chart type from the method described in Step 2.

5 In the drop-down menu that appears, select 3-D View.

6 Type here to change the elevation of the view.

You can change the number format of any of the data used in your chart. Simply select the relevant cells then choose Number from the Format menu.

7 Type here to change the degree of rotation.

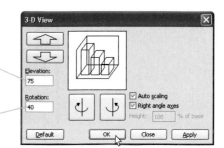

8 To change the properties of a chart element, double-click on it. Here, the font properties of the axis legends are being changed.

When changing the format of a chart, always use the bubbles that appear when you rest your cursor over a chart area. You can then be sure that you are about to format the area you mean to, before you double-click or right-click on it.

9 Click OK to apply your changes.

Importing data into a chart

To import data from an external source into a chart, make sure that it is open for editing (it will have a striped border around it, and the Microsoft Graph toolbar will be visible), then do the following:

1 Select Import File from the Edit menu.

If there is no striped border around the chart, then double-click directly on it. This will open the chart for editing.

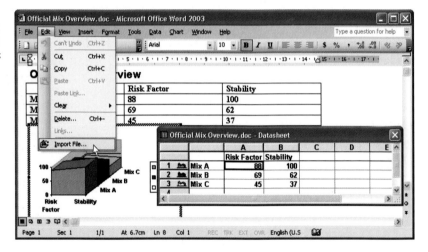

2 In the Import File dialog, select the file you want to import, then click Open.

When you are working on a chart, you are effectively using the Microsoft Graph application. This means that the menu options and toolbar icons that you see are relevant only to Microsoft Graph. To exit this mode and return to the normal Word environment, simply click your cursor anywhere outside the chart area; the Word toolbars and menu options will then return.

Web-based documents

HTML is one of Word's native file formats.

There are many features relating to the Internet and to documents intended for viewing online. Items normally present in web pages, such as hyperlinks, can be incorporated into standard Word documents allowing instant access to files stored locally or anywhere on the Internet.

Word allows automatic editing of HTML web pages using an intuitive drag-and-drop interface.

Covers

Introduction | 142

Creating a Web document | 143

Saving a Web document | 144

Frames | 145

Alternative text | 147

The Web Tools palette | 148

Adding video clips | 149

Measuring using pixels | 150

Hyperlinks | 151

Editing existing HTML files | 153

View HTML Source | 154

Chapter Twelve

Introduction

In the past, word processors were used as tools for producing pure text documents and little else. Recent years have seen popular word processors become embellished with new graphically-oriented features, which previously would have been found only in high-end desktop publishing packages.

Until recently, the aim for most people using a word processor was to produce something that would ultimately be output on paper. However, the growing importance of the Internet and Intranet environments has seen a change in this situation. Communication which was once conducted on paper is increasingly being carried out in a purely electronic medium.

This electronic communication is carried out in a variety of forms. The World Wide Web is a vast resource, containing endless linked pages, with text and pictures on virtually any topic imaginable. Until recently email had been restricted to text, and is essentially a means of communicating with a more restricted set of people.

However, these boundaries are beginning to be blurred. Word, for example, allows you to create an electronic document which is not simply text but which may contain:

- animations
- pictures
- sounds
- videos
- links to other documents or web pages

In fact, any document which you create in Word (or in any element of Microsoft Office) may be placed on the Web. You can even use Word as your primary means of composing/editing email messages.

Word also allows you to create web pages in the Web's native format, HTML (HyperText Markup Language), without having to learn the many HTML codes. Word now offers a high level of support for XML (eXtensible Markup Language), which allows documents and data to be organized and stored in a format easily shared across platforms and different types of software.

Creating a Web document

There are several ways to create a Web document.

You can also create a new Web page using this icon on the Toolbar, if visible:

1 Choose New from the File menu.

2 The Task Pane will show its New Document controls. Under the New section click Web page.

A new blank document will appear. Initially it doesn't look any different to other documents. However, when you've saved it, you'll be able to view it in a standard Web Browser.

Using Web Templates

You can also start a new document based on a Web Template.

1 In the Task Pane, choose one of the options under Templates.

2 The Templates dialog appears. Templates based on Web pages have a distinctive icon. Select one of these.

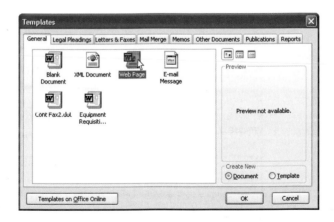

3 A new document based on a copy of the chosen Template will be created.

Saving a Web document

You can edit a Web document in the normal way. When you are ready to save it for the first time:

1 Choose Save from the File menu or click the Save icon.

2 The following dialog box will appear. Under Save as type, make sure that either Single File Web Page (*.mht; *.mhtml) or Web Page (*.htm; *.html) is selected.

A web page will typically consist of a .htm or .html file plus other files needed as resources by the web page. These other files may include graphics, sounds, or other multimedia types. If you save as a Single File Web Page (.mht or .mhtml) all this will be packaged as one file, which makes distribution easier. Note that this format is supported by Internet Explorer version 4.0 or later. If you use a different browser, then check for compatibility before using this file format.

3 Click the Change Title button to define the title as it would appear in a Web Browser.

Remember to use Web Layout view when you are working on a Web document.

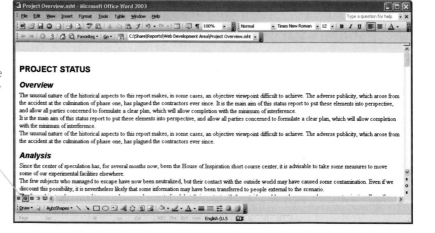

Frames

Frames allow you to divide your screen into rectangular areas, each of which can be used to view a different web page (or a different part of the same web page). In the example below we have set up two extra frames: the left frame is used for navigation while the top will show some new content.

The Frames toolbar

Create new frame to the left of the current frame

New frame to the right

New frame directly above current frame

New frame below current one

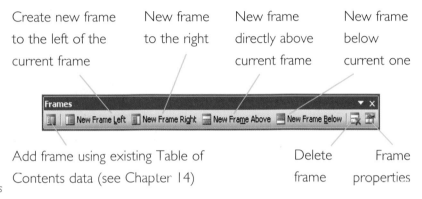

Add frame using existing Table of Contents data (see Chapter 14)

Delete frame

Frame properties

> **HOT TIP** The use of frames is not limited to web documents. Another useful tool for normal documents, often used in web pages, is the Text box (see Chapter 14 "Advanced topics").

Adding a new Frame

Here we firstly clicked Add frame using existing Table of Contents data. This uses the document's structure of Headings and Sub-headings to create the navigational links typical of many web pages. Then we clicked on the New Frame Above button to add a new frame which we'll use to display a constant header for our pages.

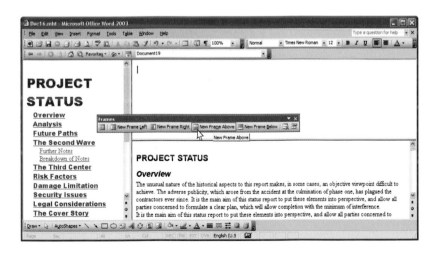

Adding text and graphics to a Frame

Once you've added a frame it behaves like an independent document: you can add/edit text or other objects as normal.

In the example below, we've inserted a picture from a file and also incorporated some WordArt.

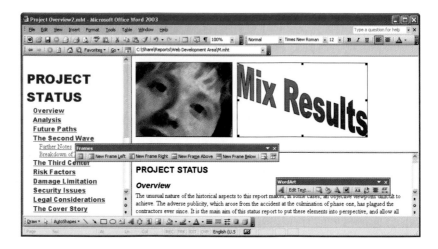

The Frame Properties dialog

1 Make sure the insertion point is somewhere inside the frame.

2 Click on the Frame Properties button in the Frames toolbar.

3 From the Frames Tab you can set the name, size and web page. From the Borders tab you can switch on the Frames border, allowing users to resize the frame.

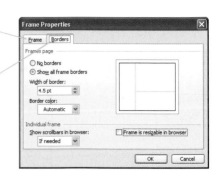

You can also access this dialog box by right-clicking inside a frame and choosing Frame Properties.

4 Click OK. In this example we have prevented the user from manually resizing the frame.

Alternative text

Remember that some web browsers do not display graphics. Also, because graphics take much longer to download from the web, a user may decide to switch off a graphic display preference. In these cases, you can set text to be displayed as an alternative.

1 Right-click on the graphic and choose Format Picture from the drop-down menu.

2 Click on the Web tab and enter the text.

Alternative text also displays while a picture is loading. You may want to include the graphic's file size to give your users an idea of how long the loading process will take.

The Web Tools palette

Word provides you with a powerful set of tools to enhance your web pages. This can be activated just like any other palette (either use the View menu or right-click on an existing Toolbar).

There is also a Web toolbar, which contains controls similar to those found in a Web Browser, e.g. forward page, back page, access favorites.

Toggle Design Mode on/off

Radio button

Add checkbox

Text box

Text area

Add Reset button

Add Sound

Hidden text

Properties

Microsoft Script Editor

Dropdown box

List box

Add Submit button

Submit image button

Add movie

Password field

Add animated scrolling text

As soon as you select one of the tools for adding objects to your web page, Word automatically activates Design Mode.

Design Mode

When Design Mode is active you can add, edit or delete objects such as radio buttons or text boxes.

When Design Mode is inactive you can test out your objects. Clicking on a check box, for example, will switch its checkmark on and off.

Microsoft Script Editor

For more details about how to write and edit scripts, refer to the Microsoft Script Editor/online Help.

This allows you to add functionality to your web page by adding scripts written in Microsoft Visual Basic® or JScript® (Java Script).

Adding video clips

Most web pages are a collection of text, images and links to other pages. However, as the multimedia capabilities of PCs increase, more types of media are becoming ever more common on the Web. For example, you can place video clips on your web pages.

1 Place the cursor where you want to insert your video.

2 Click on the Add Movie button ⊞ in the Web toolbar.

You can also add a movie to a normal document by choosing Object from the Insert menu, then selecting Windows Media Player or any other installed object capable of displaying movies.

3 Click Browse next to the Movie field, then select the video file.

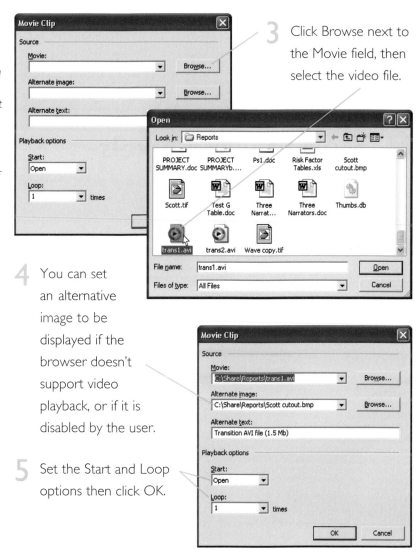

4 You can set an alternative image to be displayed if the browser doesn't support video playback, or if it is disabled by the user.

5 Set the Start and Loop options then click OK.

HOT TIP

You can alter the video size in the normal way by dragging its control handles. Be aware, however, that most video files will look best when played at their exact original size.

HOT TIP

You can use the alignment buttons on your imported video object as you would with a still image or paragraph of text.

The video clip appears at your insertion point.

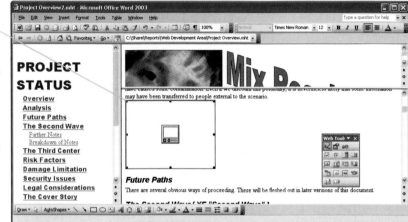

Measuring using pixels

When working with web pages, the computer screen is the primary output device. It is thus much more convenient to measure objects in pixels rather than units like centimeters, inches or points.

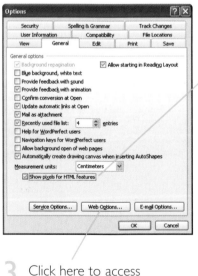

1 Choose Options from the Tools menu.

2 Click on the General tab and switch on Show pixels for HTML features.

3 Click here to access further web options.

Hyperlinks

Hyperlinks are typically used to provide a method of moving between one HTML document and another. With Word you are not restricted to using hyperlinks in HTML pages. You can place them in any normal Word document to link to another place in the same document, to another Word document on your hard drive or local network, or even to a file anywhere on the Internet/Intranet.

AutoFormatting Hyperlinks as you type

By default, Word's AutoFormat feature will automatically convert any piece of text that looks like an Internet address or other file location to a hyperlink. These addresses must be in the standard URL format, with which you will be familiar if you have experience of using a web browser.

Click on these arrows to move backwards and forwards through documents and web pages you have visited recently.

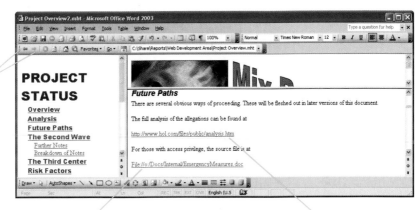

This is a link to a Word file on a hard drive accessible from the current PC. Note that the prefix "File://" is needed for Word to recognize this as a file location.

This is an Internet URL, linking to a website. In general you must be connected to the Internet for this link to work.

Inserting Hyperlinks manually

The AutoFormat method is fine for converting actual Internet addresses and file locations to hyperlinks, but many hyperlink markers do not take this format; instead the hyperlink is represented by some more meaningful text, or even an image. You can use Word to make either of these into a hyperlink.

Select the text or image that the user will click on, to jump to your linked file or website.

Click on the Insert Hyperlink icon in the Standard toolbar.

Type or select the name of the file to link to (a file or a web page). Use the browsing buttons to search for a specific location.

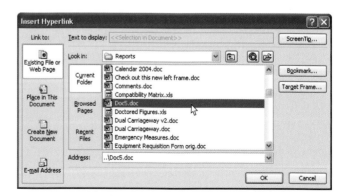

Editing existing HTML files

HTML is a native file format for Word. This means that you can open, edit and save in .htm or .html format just as easily as the .doc files more traditionally associated with Word.

Word allows you to open any HTML file, even if it was created in a different application. Any advanced HTML codes not editable by Word will be left undisturbed, so you can edit in complete safety.

Some specialist programs such as Microsoft FrontPage allow you to design web pages using advanced effects like animated buttons. You can still take the files produced by FrontPage and edit them using Word.

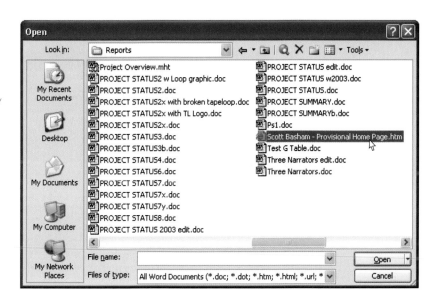

Here we've opened a file created by a separate web design package. We can now edit its text, graphics and even the hyperlinks.

If you have been editing a file which has already been saved in .htm format, you don't necessarily need to use the Save as Web Page option. A simple Save will suffice.

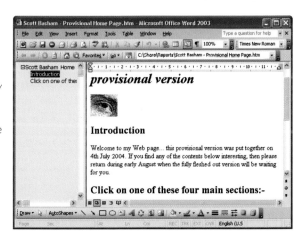

View HTML Source

If you are familiar with HTML coding, you may want to use the Microsoft Development Environment tool to edit your web page. Once you have the page open in Word simply choose HTML Source from the View menu.

1 Open up any .htm or .html web page in Word.

2 Go to the View menu and choose HTML Source.

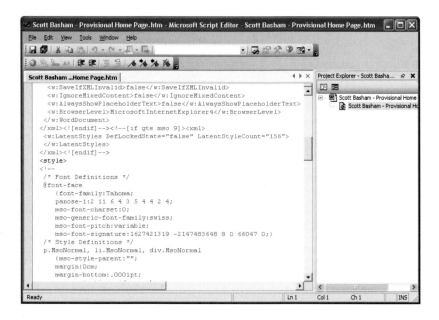

This tool scores over a straight text editor in a number of ways. It allows you to see an organized view of your web pages, and also uses a color coding system to help you distinguish the syntax.

When you install Word, its HTML Source editor is not normally included in the hard disk installation, unless you have specifically selected it using a custom install. If the editor is not installed, the first time you attempt to access the feature, Word will perform the install there and then. You may be prompted to insert one of the original Word or Office install CDs.

Working with others

Many of the recent additions to Word (and the other Microsoft Office Applications) have been designed to make working in teams easier to manage and control. If it is necessary for more than one person to work on a document, then care must be taken to ensure that everyone knows which is the definitive version. This chapter covers a range of features and techniques which are useful for collaborative work. It also looks at support for XML, which has rapidly established itself as a powerful and flexible file format used to help share data and definitions.

Covers

The Reviewing toolbar | 156

Highlighting text | 156

Inserting Comments | 157

Collaborating on documents | 158

Versioning | 159

Tracking changes | 160

Protecting a document | 162

Shared Workspaces | 163

Using XML | 164

Chapter Thirteen

The Reviewing toolbar

Word incorporates several sophisticated features that allow you to review documents clearly, and track the various stages of these reviews. The Reviewing toolbar contains icons that allow you to access these features easily. It can be displayed in the normal way from the View menu.

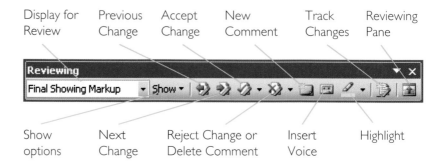

Display for Review · Previous Change · Accept Change · New Comment · Track Changes · Reviewing Pane

Show options · Next Change · Reject Change or Delete Comment · Insert Voice · Highlight

Highlighting text

If you want to mark a piece of text without adding additional notes, you can highlight it, just as if you were using a real highlighter pen on paper. To do this, follow either of the steps below:

1   Select the text then click on the Highlighter icon.

If you use the Highlighter icon's drop-down menu, you can choose from a range of colors. Selecting None will remove the highlight altogether.

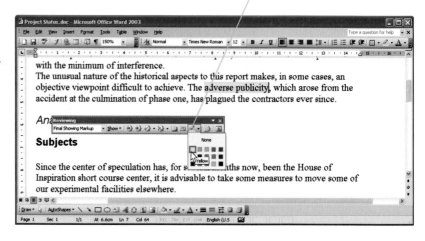

2   Alternatively, click the Highlighter first, then select any text.

Inserting Comments

To insert a comment on a section of your document:

1 Select the text on which you wish to comment.

2 Click the Insert Comment icon.

HOT TIP

If you rest the mouse over text with a comment attached for a few moments, the comment itself will appear in its own box:

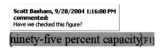

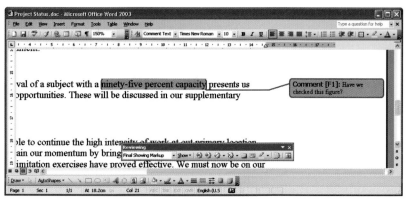

3 Enter your remarks in the comments box that appears.

4 The text is now displayed with square brackets, to remind you that there is a comment attached.

HOT TIP

You can also use the writing pad (accessed from the Languages toolbar) to add ink comments. Once these are inserted you can right-click to convert to normal comment text.

HOT TIP

As well as the pop-up text box, comments can be displayed in two ways: as "balloons" depicted in the illustration at the top of the page, or in a rectangular area at the bottom of the screen. You can switch between these methods by opening the Show menu in the Reviewing toolbar.

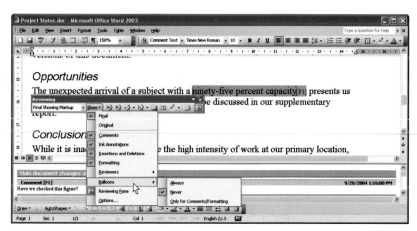

Collaborating on documents

If each of the different reviewers of a document works from a different computer, which is used by him or her alone, then there should be no need to alter the reviewer information, as this should have been established when Word was installed. However, if a computer is shared by a number of people to review documents, then the user information should be changed whenever a reviewer begins, so that it is clear who made which comments.

Select Options from the Tools menu.

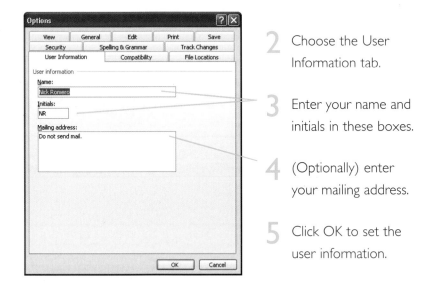

2 Choose the User Information tab.

3 Enter your name and initials in these boxes.

4 (Optionally) enter your mailing address.

5 Click OK to set the user information.

Merging documents

If a number of reviewers have been working together on the same document by updating the same Word file, then the sum of all their efforts is collected in the most up-to-date version of the document. However, if different reviewers have made changes to a document and saved the results as a different file, it is possible to merge the files back into one document.

With one file open, choose Tools>Compare and Merge Documents.

2 A file dialog appears. Double-click on the file to merge.

Versioning

You can save the various stages of a document, allowing you to see how it has developed and (if relevant) which authors have made which changes. To save a new version, do the following:

1 Go to the File menu and choose Versions.

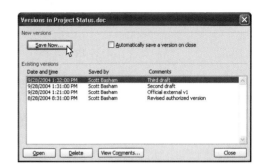

2 Click on Save Now.

3 In the dialog which appears, enter comment text for the new version, then click OK.

To review the different versions of a document, follow these steps:

1 Select Versions from the File menu.

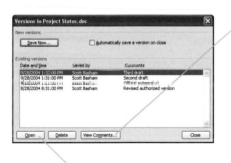

2 Select a version, then click on the View Comments button for more information on the document.

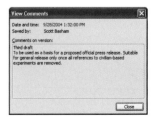

3 Click here to open the selected version of the document.

Tracking changes

Sometimes it is important to track changes you make to a document, so that someone else can see exactly what you have done. It may even be necessary for someone to approve or reject those changes before they become permanently incorporated into the document.

To start tracking changes, do the following:

1 Select the Track Changes icon in the Reviewing toolbar.

Track Changes

2 Now as you edit your document, your changes will be visibly logged. It will be easy to see exactly what has been changed.

Exactly how changes are depicted will depend on the settings you make from the Show pop-up menu in the Reviewing toolbar. In the first example, the balloons feature has been selected for all types of change. In the second example, balloons are only used for Comments/ Formatting, so ordinary text edits are shown in place.

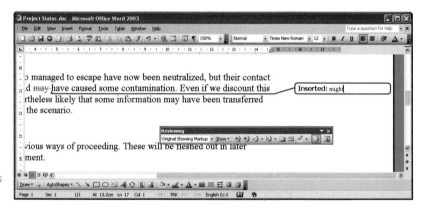

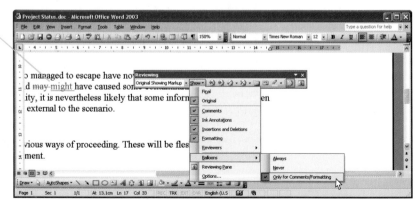

In the example below you can see a comment and also some formatting changes made to one of the headings.

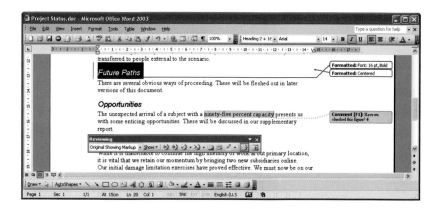

Accepting or rejecting changes

Anyone responsible for reviewing the changes in the document can do this using the Reviewing toolbar.

Use the next (or previous) button on the Reviewing toolbar to locate a change.

Choose Options from the Show menu in the Reviewing toolbar to see this dialog.

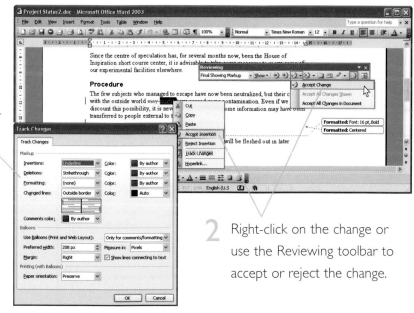

2 Right-click on the change or use the Reviewing toolbar to accept or reject the change.

Protecting a document

Word allows you to protect your document in a number of ways. You can control which aspects may be edited; for example, you might allow a user to add comments but not edit text directly. You may decide to only allow formatting via styles, thereby making sure that your document conforms to strict, consistent design guidelines.

1 Choose Protect Document from the Tools menu. The Task pane displays its Protect Document controls.

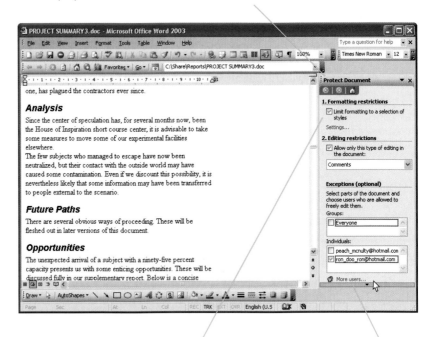

2 Select the appropriate formatting and editing restrictions before saving your document.

3 You can also specify which users or groups of users will have access to your document. Click the More users link to add or remove items from the list.

Shared Workspaces

This feature is a part of SharePoint Team Services, a Microsoft technology which allows many people to work on the same document in a controlled but flexible way. As well as sharing documents, tasks and processes can be managed within a team.

The Shared Workspace Task Pane

The SharePoint Team Services features are integrated with all the Microsoft Office applications including Excel, Access and Outlook.

1 Choose Shared Workspace from the Tools menu. The Task Pane displays the Shared Workspace set of controls.

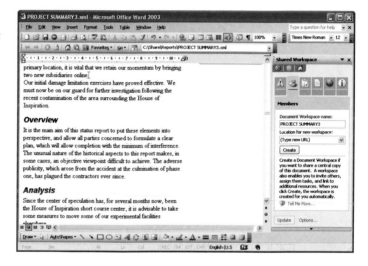

The Workspace URL should be located on a server running Microsoft SharePoint Team Services (built on Windows .NET Server technology).

2 If you have not yet set up a Document Workspace, then you can do so by specifying the URL of its location.

3 Click on the Options hyperlink near the bottom of the Task Pane to see this dialog:

Using XML

Opening and editing XML documents

XML (eXtensible Markup Language) has gained widespread support right across the computer industry. It is essentially a flexible base specification which allows developers to create a wide range of XML-based languages.

Word allows you to open any XML-based file for viewing and editing. It is easy to see the structure of tags, and make sure that the document maintains its XML validity.

1 Choose Open from the File menu and select the XML file.

This example depicts Word's generalized view of XML files. An XSLT (eXtensible Stylesheet Language Transformation) can also be used to provide a view specific to a particular XML-based language. Click here to select an XSLT to provide such a view.

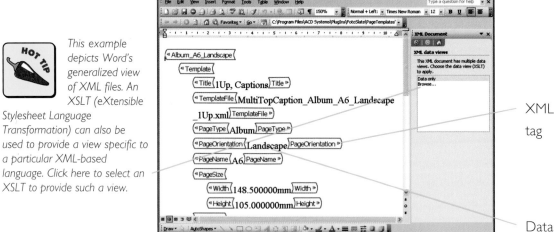

XML tag

Data

2 XML tags are easily distinguished by their curved colored boxes, with arrows to indicate whether it is an opening or closing tag.

Word also allows you to associate XSDs (XML Schema Definitions) with XML files. An XSD will describe, in full detail, a language and structure based on the XML standard. For more details on the further development of XML and its related technologies see www.w3.org, which is the home page of the World Wide Web Consortium (W3C).

The XML Task Pane

This allows you to view and navigate through the structure of an XML document.

1   Make sure the Task Pane is visible, and choose the XML Structure set of controls.

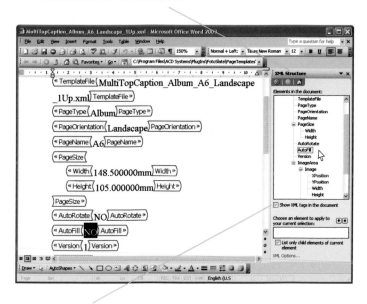

2   Click here to switch the tags on or off.

3   You can expand or collapse branches within the tree view by clicking on the + or - icons.

4   Click on an item within the tree view to move to that part of the document.

5   Click the XML Options, near the bottom of the Task Pane, to see this dialog:

6 If you click on a parent tag, its children will automatically be highlighted.

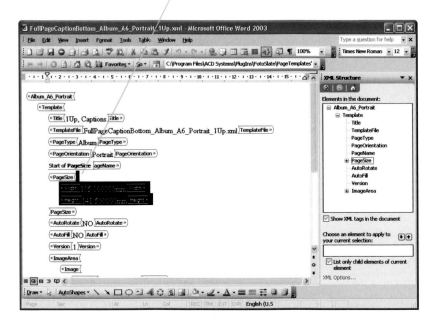

Saving a normal Word Document in XML format

You can save any normal Word documents to an XML file, which may make data sharing with other platforms and applications easier.

1 Choose Save from the File menu.

Word's XML file format supports most, but not all, of Word's features. In this example, the original Word document contained versions. A warning appears when saving as XML, reminding you that the versioning will be lost.

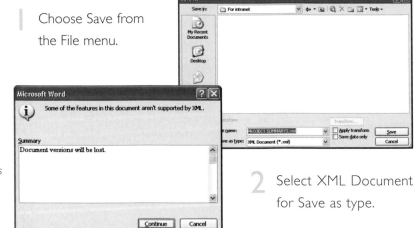

2 Select XML Document for Save as type.

Advanced topics

Word has many advanced features. Some are designed to generally make life easier, while others allow you to enhance your documents with text boxes, sound, tables of contents or even to compile an index.

Covers

Text boxes | 168

Macros | 169

Footnotes and Endnotes | 171

Tables of Contents | 172

Bookmarks | 177

Indexing | 178

Adding sound | 181

Language Autodetect | 182

The Research Pane | 183

Compatibility options | 186

Installing features | 186

Chapter Fourteen

Text boxes

When you click on the Text Box icon in the Drawing toolbar your cursor will turn into a cross symbol.

Text boxes give independent control over text flow/positioning.

Inserting a new Text box

1 Click on the Text box icon in the Drawing Toolbar.

2 Click and drag diagonally to create the Text Box.

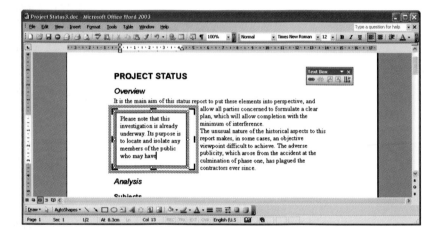

3 Click inside the box to enter or edit the text within. You can move the box by dragging on its edge, and resize by dragging on one of its handles.

The Text box toolbar
This gives you access to additional text box options.

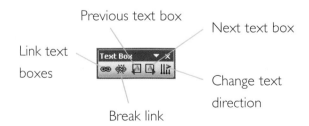

Previous text box

Next text box

Link text boxes

Change text direction

Break link

To create linked Text boxes

1 Click on the first text box.

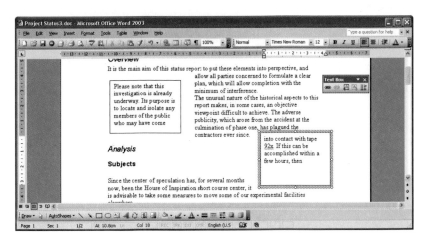

2 Click on the Link button in the Text Box toolbar.

3 Click on the second text box. Any text which doesn't fit in the first box will now flow automatically into the second.

Macros

Macros are recordings of common activities. You can record your own macros, and play them back whenever necessary.

You can also access macro recording and playback by opening the Tools menu and choosing Macros.

Recording a Macro

1 Go to the View menu, choose Toolbars and make sure that the Visual Basic Toolbar is active.

This contains buttons for recording and replaying macros.

Run Macro   Record Macro   Visual Basic Editor (for editing macros on a command-by-command basis)

Macro names must begin with a letter and can contain up to 80 letters and numbers. Spaces or special characters are not allowed.

2 When you click the Record Macro button the following dialog box appears. Enter a name for your macro.

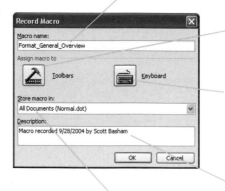

3 Click here to assign your new macro to a toolbar.

4 Click here to assign your new macro to a keyboard shortcut.

5 Select the template where you want to store the macro.

6 Enter a description for your macro.

You can also stop macro recording by opening the Tools menu and choosing Macros.

7 When you click OK, recording becomes active. You can now "walk" through the commands you wish to be included in the macro. During this time your cursor takes the form of a pointer with a cassette tape attached. There is also a small toolbar which allows you to pause or stop recording:

8 When you have finished recording, click the Stop icon.

Running a Macro

You can run a macro from a toolbar icon or keyboard shortcut if you chose either of those options when creating the macro.

1 To play back a macro, click the Play button and choose your macro from the dialog box.

2 Click Run.

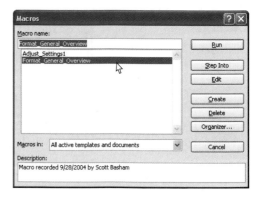

Footnotes and Endnotes

Word allows you to add footnotes (which appear at the bottom of a page), or endnotes (at the end of your document). These reference text on the main page, usually using a superscript number.

1 Select the text which will reference the footnote or endnote. Choose Footnote from the Insert menu, Reference submenu.

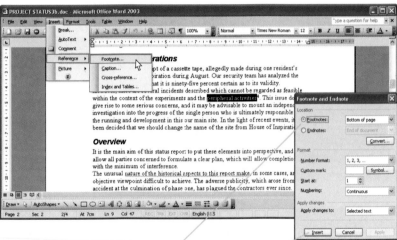

2 Choose Footnotes/Endnotes, select a Numbering option, then click Insert.

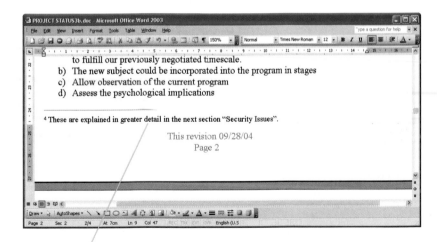

3 You can now enter the text for your footnote or endnote.

Tables of Contents

You can automatically create a Table of Contents by asking Word to look for instances of particular styles, or by using entries that you create manually. Word will track each entry's page numbers.

Creating a new Table of Contents

1 Place your insertion point at a suitable location for your Table of Contents.

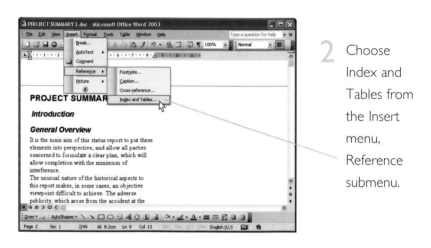

2 Choose Index and Tables from the Insert menu, Reference submenu.

3 Make sure the Table of Contents tab is active.

4 Set the page and tab options.

5 Apply a style from the Formats drop-down list then click OK.

By default Word will use instances of the styles Heading 1, 2, and 3 to build the Table of Contents. You can change this by clicking on the Options button.

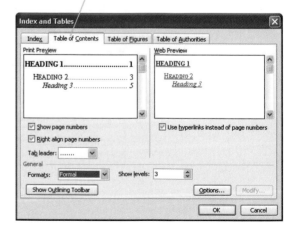

Word scans through your document for instances of different heading styles, and creates the Table of Contents.

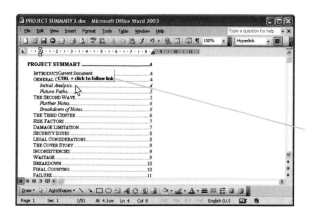

The entries in the Table are hyperlinks to the actual pages. Hold down the Control key and click on an entry to jump to that part of the document.

Updating a Table of Contents

In Layout view, a gray background on the Table of Contents indicates that you're looking at a Word Field. Fields contain text which Word automatically generates. The background doesn't print, but you can change it by selecting Options from the Tools menu. Click on the View tab and choose a different option under Field shading.

If you have added new headings, or edited your document so that the page numbers are different, then you'll probably want to update the Table of Contents to reflect the changes.

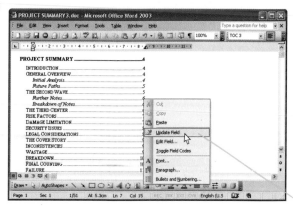

If you have added or removed headings or Table of Contents entries, then you will need to choose Update entire table.

1 Right-click on the Table of Contents and choose Update Field from the drop-down menu.

2 Decide whether to update just the page numbers or to rebuild the whole table.

Any new entries now appear in the Table of Contents, and the page numbering is back in sync with the document.

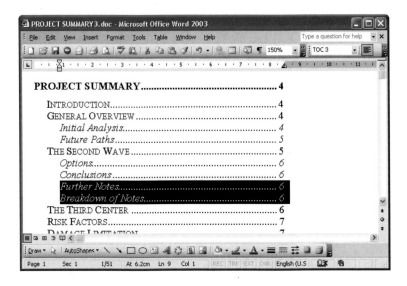

Altering the appearance of the Table of Contents

Once the Table of Contents has been created, you can apply formatting in the normal way.

Entries in the Contents Table use special styles which Word sets up automatically (they are named "TOC" plus a level number). Any formatting changes you make normally affect these styles. This means that the new formatting will be retained even if you rebuild the Table of Contents.

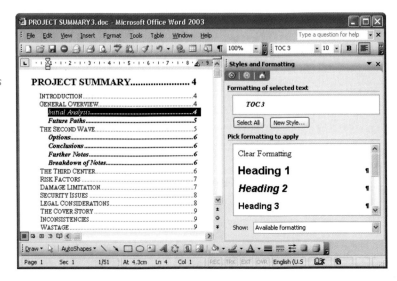

Adding a manual entry to the Table of Contents

Sometimes you may want to add an entry which does not use one of the Heading styles.

| Click in the relevant text. Choose Field from the Insert menu.

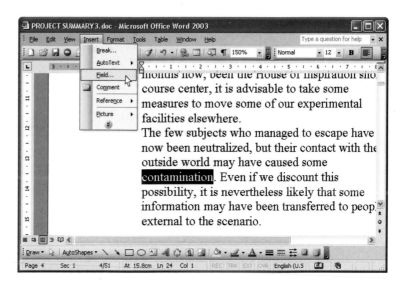

2 Under Categories, choose Index and Tables. For field names choose TC.

3 Add the text for the entry here.

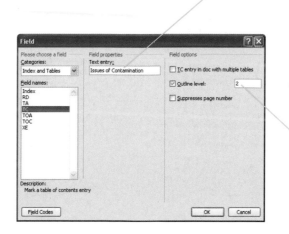

4 To set the entry at a particular level in the table, enter the level number here.

The field for the TOC entry is added to your document.

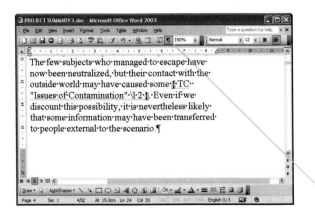

Normally the TOC field isn't visible in your document. To display hidden characters and fields, click on this button.

5 To rebuild the Table of Contents, click to select your existing table, then choose Insert>Reference>Index and Tables.

6 In the Index and Tables dialog, click the Options button.

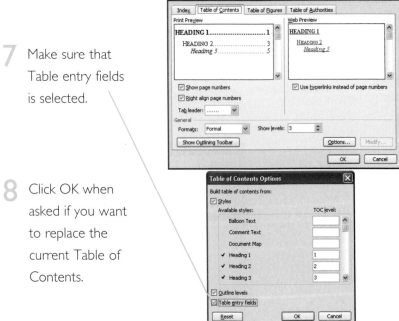

7 Make sure that Table entry fields is selected.

8 Click OK when asked if you want to replace the current Table of Contents.

Bookmarks

A Bookmark can help you keep track of a location in your document.

1 To create a Bookmark, place your insertion point, then choose Bookmark from the Insert menu.

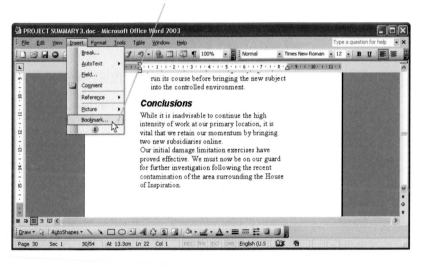

2 Enter a name for your Bookmark then click the Add button.

3 To go to a bookmark, open the Edit menu and choose Go To. In the dialog which appears enter your bookmark name or select from the pop-up menu.

Bookmarks can be used to let you specify a range of pages when creating an index entry. See Page 179 for more details.

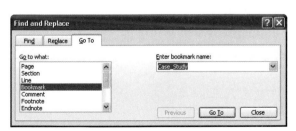

Indexing

Word makes the process of creating an index fairly straightforward.

Adding an Index entry

1 Select the text to be made into an entry.

2 Choose Index and Tables from the Insert menu, Reference submenu.

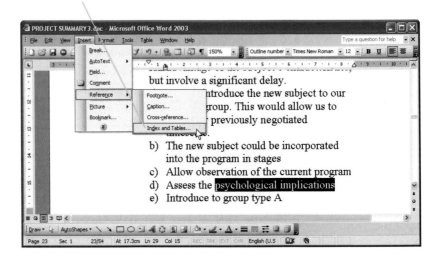

The Mark Index Entry dialog stays open even after you've clicked the Mark button. This means that you can create another index entry (by scrolling through your main document then clicking the Mark button again), without having to go back through the menus.

3 Click on the Mark Entry button.

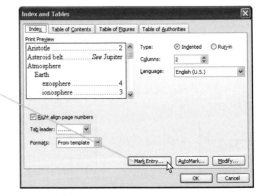

4 If necessary, edit the text inserted in Main entry.

5 For a simple entry, leave the options set at Current Page and click on Mark.

Topics and Subtopics

Most entries will probably only need to have text in the Main entry part of this dialog box.

See the next page for an example of subtopics in an actual index.

However, if you want an index which includes topics and subtopics, fill in the main topic under Main entry, then the subtopic under Subentry.

Specifying ranges of pages

For most index entries you'll want just a single page number to appear. If you want a range of pages:

You can also create cross-reference entries. Click on the Cross-reference option and type in the relevant text for the entry.

1 Move to the end of the topic and create a bookmark (see Page 177).

2 Locate the start of the topic and mark the index entry. Set the Options to Page range, and set the end by choosing the bookmark from the drop-down list.

Generating the Index

1   Click where you'd like the Index to appear. Go to the Insert
    menu and choose Index and Tables.

2   Make sure the Index tab is active.

3   Select an
    index type,
    number of
    columns and
    format, then
    click OK.

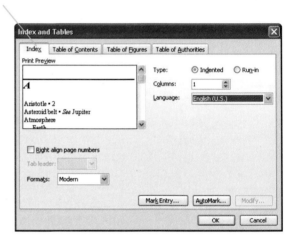

An example Index

Main topic   Subtopic

*As with the Table
of Contents, you
can rebuild the
index at any time,
or change its
formatting by editing the styles
(each is named "Index" followed
by a level number).*

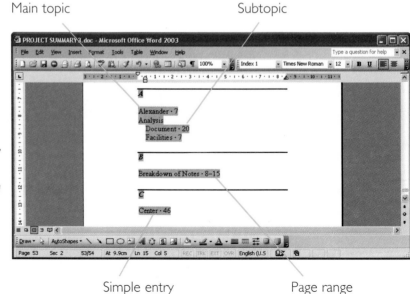

Simple entry   Page range

Adding sound

You can add background music or sound recordings to a web page document just as easily as adding the video clip (see Chapter 12).

Word allows you to use files in a number of formats including WAV and MIDI. Whenever someone accesses your page, this file is played, assuming the browser allows background music, and a suitable driver for the type of sound file has been installed.

If the Web Toolbar is not visible go to the View menu, choose Toolbars then Web Tools. Alternatively right-click on any visible toolbar to see the pop-up menu.

1 Click on the Sound icon in the Web toolbar:

2 Click Browse.

3 Select the required sound file then click Open.

4 Set the looping option then click OK.

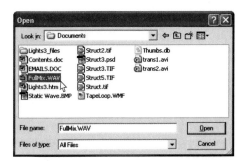

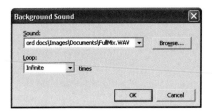

In this example, the file FullMix.WAV will play and repeat indefinitely as long as the user is on the current web page.

Note that you can add a sound file to any Word document (not just Web pages) by choosing Object from the Insert menu. Wave sound and MIDI sequence are just two examples of the files you are able to import.

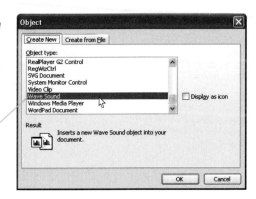

Language Autodetect

If you have multiple languages installed, Word can automatically select the correct language based on what you're currently typing. This means that features such as the Spelling Checker and Thesaurus will use the correct dictionary.

Installing multiple languages

If you only have one language currently installed, you will need to install at least one more for the Language Autodetect feature to have anything to do.

1 Click on the Windows Start button, choose Programs>Microsoft Office>Microsoft Office Tools>Microsoft Office 2003 Language Settings.

2 To add a language, select it from the list on the left and click Add. Continue for any other languages then click OK or Apply.

When you change the Microsoft Office Language Settings, Windows usually needs to shut down any Microsoft Office applications such as Word. A dialog box will appear, offering to do this for you automatically.

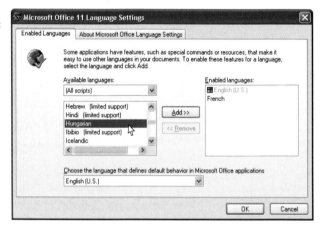

You can also manually specify a language for any block of text. To do this, simply select the text, then choose Tools>Language>Set Language and click on the desired language.

3 Back in Word choose Tools>Language>Set Language. Make sure that Detect language automatically is switched on.

The Research Pane

The Task pane now incorporates a new set of controls grouped under the heading Research. Research covers automatic translation, a thesaurus and access to information sources across the Web.

Automatic translation

1 Select the text then choose Tools>Language>Translate.

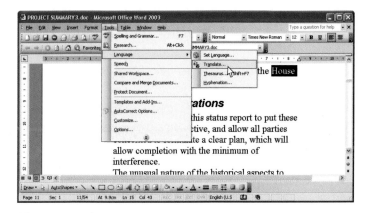

2 The Translate section of the Task Pane appears. Choose the destination language, then click Go.

The translation feature works better on single words rather than whole sentences or paragraphs. Do not completely rely on automatic translation services; you will usually be surprised (and sometimes entertained) if you translate back into English and compare the text with the original.

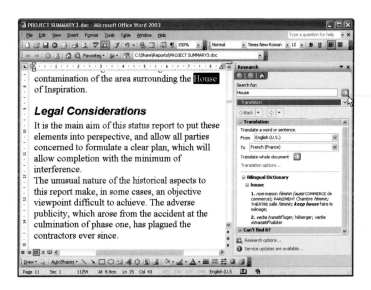

Searching for synonyms

Word lets you search for synonyms while you're editing the active document. You do this by calling up Word's resident Thesaurus. The Thesaurus categorizes words into meanings; each meaning is allocated various synonyms from which you can choose.

As a bonus, the Thesaurus also supplies antonyms. For example, if you look up "good" in the Thesaurus, Word lists "poor" as an antonym.

Using the Thesaurus

1   Select the word for which you require a synonym or antonym.

2   Choose Tools>Language>Thesaurus. The Research Pane will open displaying its Thesaurus controls.

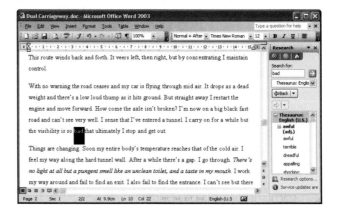

3   If you move the mouse over any of the listed suggestions, you will be able to access a pop-up menu allowing you to insert the item, copy to the Clipboard, or even look up this item in the Thesaurus.

More general Research

Once the Research pane is visible, you can easily access a variety of sources both locally and across the Web.

A quick way to access the Research pane is to Alt+click on a word in your document. The Research pane will open using whatever set of controls (e.g. Thesaurus) you used most recently. A lookup will be made on the word you clicked.

1   If you have text in your document which you want to use as keyword(s) in your research, then select it.

2   Choose Tools>Research.

3   Select the Research source(s) from this pop-up menu.

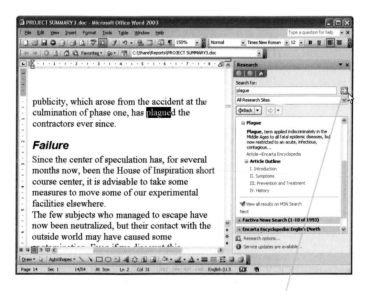

4   If the search has not already run, then click this button. You can also use this to refresh the search if you decide to edit the Search for text.

5   If you click the Research options hyperlink (near the bottom of the Task pane) this dialog appears:

Compatibility options

These settings only affect how Word displays a document which has been saved in a particular format. They do not permanently change its formatting.

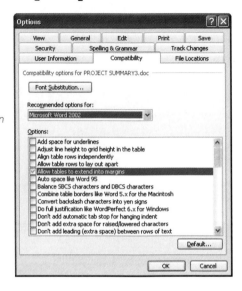

You can customize how Word displays documents which have been saved in another format.

1　Choose Options in the Tools menu.

2　Click on the Compatibility tab, select a format and view or change its options.

Installing features

In order to conserve hard disk space, you can choose to include only the commonly used features when you first install Word. Later on, if you try to use a feature which isn't installed, Word will ask if you want to load it there and then. If you answer Yes, you'll need to insert your original CD.

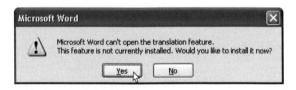

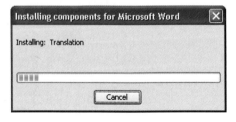

Once the installation has been completed you'll be able to use the newly installed feature.

Index

A

Accepting or rejecting changes   161
Add movie button   148
Alignment   36, 150
Animated buttons   153
Animated scrolling text   148
Antonyms   184
Arrow   116
Auto Recover   25
AutoComplete   97
AutoCorrect   94
    Options   18
AutoFormat   70
Automatic customization   15
AutoShapes   118
AutoSum   135
AutoSummarize   94
AutoText   95
Axis   139

B

Backspace key   21
Bitmapped objects   110
Blank Document template   100
BMP files   110
Bold   23, 33
Bookmarks   177
Border Color   135
Bounding rectangle   114
Breaking down elements   114
Brightness   113
Bubbles
    Chart area indicators   139
Building a drop-down list   103
Bulleted paragraphs   37
    Advanced   38
    Graphic bullets   39
Buttons   13

C

Calendar Wizard   107
Canvas   112
Capitalization   18
CGM files   110
Change
    Accept or Reject   156
Change shape   122
Character spacing   35
    Changing   122
Microsoft Graph Chart   137
Charts
    3-D Views   139
    Creating   137
    Formatting   138
    Importing data into   140
Checkbox   148
Checkmarks   104
Click and Type   24, 111
Clip Art   27, 111
Clip Organizer   111
Clipboard   27, 51
    Clear all   53
    Paste All   53
Collaborating on documents   158
Color   116
Column boundaries   125
Column or row boundary   125
Column width   128
Columns   56
    Balancing   57
    Breaks   57
    Mixed layout   56
Combining elements   120
Combining text and graphics   119
Commands
    Drawing-related   116
Comments   157
Compatibility   186
Compress pictures   113
Contacts
    Online   18
Tables of Contents   172–177
    Adding a manual entry to   175
    Creating   172
    Formats   172
    Options   176
    Updating   173
Contrast   113
Control handles   150
Converting text to tables   125
Copy   51
Copy and paste   52

Copying style changes   106
Creating a new document   27
Cut and paste   50

D

Dash   116
Datasheets   138
Defaults   101
Delete key   21
Deleting text   21
Design guidelines   162
Design mode   148
Diagonal table lines   126
Diagram   116
Dictating text   77
Distributing evenly
    Columns   135
    Rows   135
Document
    Structure   11
Document editing
    Preventing users from editing   104
Document Map   12, 62
Document Recovery. *See* Auto Recover
Document Window   20
Documents
    Properties   61
.DOT file type   105
Double-headed arrow   124
Download time   147
Draw Table tool   130, 135
Draw-type objects   110
Drawings   116
DRW files   110

E

Edit Picture   114
Endnotes. *See* Footnotes and Endnotes
Enhanced MetaFile   114
EPS files   110
Eraser tool   135
Expanding table cells   127

F

Faxes   107
Field names
    TC   175
File links   151
File size   147
Files created in HTML editors   153
Filling out values
    Within a form   103
Find and Replace   86–90
    Attributes   88
First-line indent   50
Font information
    Embedded in templates   101
Fonts   32
    Dialog box   34
    Printer   33
    TrueType   33
Footers   58
Footnotes and Endnotes   171
Form Fields
    Check Box   104
    Drop-Down   103
    Text   102
Form templates   102
Format AutoShape   117
Format Painter   60
Formatting   27
    Character-level   32
    Comments   160
    Paragraph-level   36
    Rows and columns   128
    Text   31–46
    Toolbar   32
Forms
    Protecting   104
Forms palette   102
Formulae   131
Frames   145
    Properties   145
Free floating palettes   138

G

GIF files   110
Global styles   106
Grammar. *See* Spelling and Grammar checking
Graphical features   109–122
Graphics
    Changing object order   119
    Creating shapes   117
    Cropping   113
    Editing   114
    Fill and Line   117

Format Picture dialog   116
Grouping and ungrouping   120
Handles   112
Manipulating   112
Tables within   136
Wrapping text around   115
Graphics tablet   26
Graphs   137

H

Handwriting text   26
Headers   145
Headers and footers   14, 58
Headings   11, 145
Help   16
Hidden text   148
Highlighting text   156
HTML   141
Editing existing files   153
View source   154
Hyperlinks   17, 151
Images   152
Hyphenation   46, 98

I

Icon
Align center   36
Align left   36
Align right   36
AutoText   95
Bold   33
Bullets   37
Chart   137
Chart types   138
Copy   51
Cut   51
Datasheet   138
Form field options   102–103
Ink   26
Italic   33
Justified   36
New document   20, 100
New web page   143
Numbering   40
Open   28
Paragraph symbols   10, 80
Paste   51
Print   29
Print preview   29
Protect form   104
Save   28
Sound   181
Spelling and grammar   92–93

Table   124
Tables and borders   135
Text box   168
Track changes   160
Underline   33
WordArt   121
Image control   113
Indents   42, 44
Indexing   178–180
Adding an index entry   178
Cross-reference   179
Example   180
Generating   180
Mark entry dialog   178
Ranges of pages   179
Topics and subtopics   179
Ink notes   26
Insert
Diagram   116
Mode   22
Object   181
Table   124
Insertion point   20
Install CD   186
Installing features   154, 186
Intelligent templates   107
Internal table lines   132
Italic   33

J

Java Script/JScript   148
JPG files   110
Justified text   36

K

Kerning   35
Keywords
For clipart objects   111

L

Landscape   14
Language Autodetect   182
Language bar   26
Left indent   50
Line
Style   135
Weight   135
Line breaks   20, 46, 98

Line spacing   45
Lines and fills   117
Link to file option   110
Linking text boxes   168
Locking a document   105

M

Macros   169
Magnification. *See* Zooming
Mail merge   27
Margins   14, 45
Maximize   49
Menus   9
    Customizing   15
Merging documents   158
Microphone wizard   76
Microsoft Script Editor   148
MIDI   181
Multimedia file types   144
Multiple languages   182
Multiple text selection   25

N

Naming a template   105
Navigation   12
Navigational links   145
.NET Server technology   163
New document controls   100
New document icon   20
Non-destructive editing   113
Normal template   106
Numbered paragraphs   40
    Advanced   41

O

Office Online   111
Online documents   141
Opening a document   28
Orphans   46
Outline numbered lists   42
Oval   116
Overtype mode   22

P

Page
    Breaks   46, 55, 98
    Layout   14
    Setup   14
    Views   10
        Normal   10
        Outline   11
        Print Layout   11
        Reading Layout   12
        Web Layout   10
    Width   49
Page numbers
    Automatic   59
Paper size   14
Paragraph dialog box   44, 46
Paragraph symbols   10
Password field   148
Paste   50
Line patterns   117
PCT files   110
PCX files   110
Pencil icon   125
Perimeter table lines   132
Pictures from disk   110
Pixels   150
Pocket PC   26
Points   45
Portrait   14
Preview/Properties   111
Previewing effects
    Text and graphic   11
Printing   30
    Preview   29
Protecting a document   105, 162

R

Radio button   148
Redo   54
Replace. *See* Find and Replace
Replacing text   22, 90
Research   27
    General   185
Research Pane   183–185
Reset button   148
Reset picture   113
Resizing frames   146
Resizing windows   49
Restore windows   49
Review   156
Rotation   113
Row height   128
Ruler   9, 50

S

Saving a document   28
Screen resolution   12
Scroll bars   9
Scrolling   48
Search settings   16
Searching
    For Clip Art   111
    For text. See Find and Replace
Sections   55
Selecting text   22
Send to back   119
Shading Color   135
Shadow   116
Shared computers   158
Shared Workspaces   163
SharePoint Team Services   163
Sharing data   166
Show drawing canvas   114
Size readout   124
Smart Tags   18
Sorting
    Within tables   135
Sound   181
Special characters   91
Special graphical effects   121
Speech Recognition   75–78
    Correcting errors   78
    Preparing   76
Spelling and Grammar checking   92
Spike   96
Spreadsheets   131
Square text wrap   115
Starting a document
    From scratch   20
    Using a template   100
Starting Word   9
Status bar   9
Style dialog   106
Styles   27
    Applying a style   64
    Character-level   69
    Creating   66
    Dialog box   67
    Displaying names   74
    Editing   65
    Gallery   72
    Modifying   68
    Paragraph-level   64
    Using default styles   64
Styles and Formatting   43
Styles and Themes   63–74
Sub-headings   145
Submit button   148
Submit image button   148
Sum function
    Example   131
Synonyms   184

T

Tab stops   50
Table AutoFormat   135
Table properties
    Dialog box   130
Tables
    AutoFormat   134
    Borders and shading   132
    Controlling height and width   130
    Creating charts   137
    Cutting and pasting cells   129
    Drawing   125
    Entering text   127
    Fills   133
    Font   134
    Formatting   128
    Formulae   131
    Graphics within tables   136
    Inserting a row/column   128
    Inserting a table   124
    Irregular tables   127
    Merging cells   129
    Nested   130
    Sorting   135
    Text wrap   136
Tables and charts   123–140
Tabulation   79–84
    Bar Tabs   83
    Creating   80
    Creating tables   84
    Default   80
    Deleting   81
    Different types   81
    Tabs dialog box   83
Task Pane   9, 13, 17, 27, 143, 183
    Clipboard   53
    Formatting with   43
    Research   183
    Styles and Formatting   67
Templates
    Defaults   101
    Form   102
    Normal and general   100
    Setting up new   105
    Using   100
Templates and Add-Ins
    Dialog   106
Templates and Wizards   99–108
Text
    Area   148
    Boxes   148, 168
    Effects   35
    Flow   169
    Layer   119
    Manipulation   19–30
    Shapes   122
    Size   23
Text direction
    In tables   135
Themes   71

Thesaurus   184
Thumbnails icon   12
TIF files   110
Change Title   144
Title bar   9
Toolbars   9, 13
    Customizing   13, 15
    Drawing   116
    Header and footer   58
    Language bar   77–78
    Picture   113
    Reviewing   156
    Tables and Borders   135
    Text box   168
Tracking changes   160
Automatic translation   183
Transparent color   113

Underline   33
Undo and Redo   54
Updating fields   131
URL format   151
Users and groups   162

Versioning   159
Video clips   149
View icons   9
View menu   13
Views
    Normal   10
    Outline   11
    Print Layout   11, 24
    Reading Layout   12
    Web Layout   10, 24
Visual Basic   148, 169
Voice   156
Voice Commands   78

W3C   164
WAV   181
Web browser   10
Web documents
    Alternative text   147
    Creating   143
    Saving   144
Web pages   141
Web Templates
    Using   143
Web Tools palette   148
Web-based documents   141–154
Weight   135
Widows and Orphans   46
Windows Media Player   149
Windows MetaFile   114
Windows System Tray   53
Wizards   107–108. *See* Templates and Wizards
    Back button   108
    Finish button   108
    Next button   107
WMF files   110
WordArt   121
Working with others   155–166
World Wide Web   142
WPG files   110
Writing Pad   157. *See also* Handwriting text

XLS files
    Importing from   140
XML   142, 155, 164–166
    Opening and editing documents   164
    Options   165
    Structure   165
    Task Pane   165
    Word file format   166
XSD   164
XSLT   164

Zooming   49